DATE DUE

DEMCO 38-296

Way Off Broadway

Way Off Broadway

*A Complete Guide to Producing
Musicals with School
and Community Groups*

by
LYNN M. SOEBY

McFarland & Company, Inc., Publishers
Jefferson, North Carolina, and London

MT955 .S63 1991
Soeby, Lynn M., 1954–
Way off Broadway : a
complete guide to producing
musicals with school and
community groups

British Library Cataloguing-in-Publication data are available

Library of Congress Cataloguing-in-Publication Data

Soeby, Lynn M., 1954–
  Way off Broadway : a complete guide to producing musicals with
school and community groups / by Lynn M. Soeby.
    p. cm.
  Includes bibliographical references and index.
  ISBN 0-89950-629-1 (sewn softcover : 55# alk. paper) ∞
  1. Musicals—Production and direction. I. Title.
  MT955.S63 1991
  792.6—dc20   91-52744
                                                          CIP
                                                          MN

Manufactured in the United States of America

McFarland & Company, Inc., Publishers
  Box 611, Jefferson, North Carolina 28640

For my friend, Jack Ehrlich
whose particular brand of idealism
both infuriates and inspires me
yet, always spurs me on
in my quest for artistic expression.

And for Meredith
whose partnership and friendship
enabled me to reach higher
than I could ever have reached alone.

I love you both.

Preface and Acknowledgments

This book is about the art and craft of staging musical theatre with school and community groups. It is for the director, producer, choreographer, designer, stage manager, conductor, actor, singer, dancer, audience member or anyone with an interest in musical theatre. It is intended to be a practical guide.

In my quest for knowledge on the subject, I note a definite lack of literature and what little I have found is sketchy and often impractical. Most texts on theatre deal with the musical as an afterthought, an eccentric cousin of "real" theatre which must be invited to dinner but never asked to sit at the head table. These texts completely fail to recognize the musical for what it is: the most popular and profitable form of American theatre.

In *Way Off Broadway,* I apply the theories and practices of conventional theatre to the musical. I have underscored the text throughout with events from my experience. To gain practical knowledge, I had to make all the mistakes that were *not* in the book! I share them with you in hopes that you may avoid them.

To my family in North Dakota for their endless, loving support; my extended family in Rockport, Texas, for putting up with my "creative crazies" for eight years; my good friends in Reno, Nevada, for their encouragement over the long haul; my compadres at San Francisco State for "jump-starting" my creative juices; and Hurricane Hugo and the people of Boone and Blowing Rock, North Carolina, who "adopted" me in the final weeks of writing *Way Off Broadway:*
I thank you. This project could not have been possible without you!

Table of Contents

III. Go . . . !

Introduction

My first experience in musical theatre was as the "Mirror on the Wall" in a production of *Snow White and the Seven Dwarfs*. I can't recall the staging, lyrics to the songs, or who directed the show. I don't think it was a very good production and I don't think I was a particularly good "Mirror on the Wall," yet, the experience touched me. I was nine.

Your interest in musical theatre likely has similar beginnings. Whether as performer or viewer, curtain puller or set painter, sooner or later, we all get caught up in the magic. The curtain opens on a fascinating scene, a faraway place. Colorful characters unfold an intriguing story. Presto! Scenes change, characters transform, story evolves, audience is moved—an illusion is created.

Yet anyone who has stepped through the proscenium arch knows that a Chinese fire drill is occurring in the wings, inches from the audience—a frantic, but organized chaos borne of months of planning, weeks of rehearsal, thousands of dollars, countless stitches, swipes of the paintbrush, and legal pads full of scribbling.

The staging of a musical is a monumental task. Should you decide to attempt it, be ready to make a substantial mental, physical and emotional investment. Prepare to alienate family and friends, neglect your job, ignore your health, and postpone all other responsibilities. You'll need stores of patience, energy, imagination, single-mindedness, courage and optimism. It is character-building stuff and it will cost you plenty. Why do it? The payoff is great. It comes in a unique currency called personal satisfaction. It can make you rich.

"There's no business like show business..."
Irving Berlin, **Annie Get Your Gun**

In the following chapters you will find step-by-step practical advice on

1

the staging of a musical. I've included sections on budgeting, scheduling, casting, analyzing, staging, rehearsing, performing, promoting, costuming, lighting and building. I have tried to include every possible aspect of production. The success of your show is not based on magic but on specific knowledge, long preparation, strict organization, and tremendous hard work. Theatre is an art *and* a science. Although it may not make you a better artist, I hope this book will help you improve your craft.

I. On Your Mark...

There are many things to be considered before you begin the actual rehearsal process for a musical. This extensive planning period can last months. It is both exhaustive and exhilarating. And, it is necessary. Time and energy that you expend in preparation will ensure smooth sailing for your show.

1 Let's Do a Show!

Choosing a Show

The first step in producing a musical is choosing a show. You may have always wanted to do a production of *Hair* or stage *West Side Story*. However, if you live in a conservative rural area or if most of your prospective cast is of Nordic extraction, these may not be your best choices.

There are many things to consider in this decision-making process. Here are some questions to ask yourself as you examine various shows for possible production.

What Is My Budget?

Staging a musical is the most expensive undertaking in the realm of theatre. The royalties, rental fees, sets, costumes, lighting, sound, cost of facilities and various other costs can easily run into thousands of dollars, even in school or community theatre productions.

If you're a veteran theatre organization and in the "black," perhaps you can afford to stage a spectacle with a cast of thousands. Usually this is not the case. School productions are on a tight budget and young community groups are often struggling to pay for facilities and they cannot afford to stage an expensive show. In fact, many community groups do not even attempt musicals for this reason.

There are, however, many shows which can be successfully staged by community and school groups. Keep the following in mind as you consider shows:

SIZE OF CAST: A show with a chorus of 60 and 14 principals obviously costs more than a show with a total cast of 20.

COSTUMES: *Hello Dolly!* with its lavish 1890's period costumes would cost more to produce than *Godspell* with its 60's street look.

SETS AND SCENERY: Some shows call for a realistic set and many changes of scenery—*The Music Man, Oliver!* and *Fiddler on the Roof,* while others can be staged on a single set—*A Chorus Line, Godspell,* and *A Funny Thing Happened on the Way to the Forum.*

ROYALTIES AND MUSIC RENTAL: Generally, older shows cost less than newer shows, and some shows, such as the Gilbert and Sullivan operettas, are in the public domain—that is, there are no royalty fees to produce the show. (Note: There are fees for new versions such as the recent revival of *The Pirates of Penzance.*)

Creative budgeting and wise use of resources have enabled many a group to stage their favorite show. However, it is wise to consider finances *before* you choose a show as you won't want to consume time and energy worrying about it during production and very few shows ever come in under budget.

Who Is My Audience?

This is a most important consideration in choosing a musical. You can always scrape together more money, recruit a few more singers, find another violinist, or make do with existing facilities. Your audience is the one thing you have no control over. They come to you with a fixed set of values and expectations. Whether rural or metropolitan, sophisticated or naive, your audience may expect what you do to fit in with their way of thinking.

You must make judgments about what material is acceptable in your community. When considering scripts, pay close attention to content. You can't afford to be too idealistic.

A personal experience showed me just that. My school-sponsored community choir group elected to do the rock-opera *Jesus Christ Superstar.* We spent months in the planning stages, held auditions, and were three weeks into rehearsals when a small but vocal group voiced objections at a school board meeting. We were cancelled within the week.

"You got trouble, my friends..."
Meredith Willson, **The Music Man**

Luckily, we were able to reorganize as a nonprofit community theatre group and stage the show anyway. It was a great success.

In choosing the show, it never occurred to us that this could happen. We assumed that a twenty-year-old controversy could not affect us. Of course we were wrong. Most of the dissenters had never seen the show, read the script or heard the music. They had preconceived ideas about the show. A tough lesson, it taught me to always consider my audience.

What Are the Cast Requirements?
What Local Talent Is Available?

The excitement of thinking you have the perfect person to play the lead in a particular show sometimes leads to tunnel vision about other shows. Yes, consider your talent, but don't let that be your only criterion. As you look at shows, consider the following:

GENDER REQUIREMENTS: Some shows require many men as in *Guys and Dolls, Damn Yankees* and *Jesus Christ Superstar.* In small communities, there may be a shortage of male actors especially dancers. If this is the case in your community, don't choose a show requiring lots of men. Even if you're resourceful, you won't want to be frantically searching at the last minute. I have been known to recruit complete strangers from a nearby table in a restaurant, but I wouldn't recommend it.

AGE REQUIREMENTS: Choose a show that calls for a cast in the approximate age range of your group. *Bye Bye Birdie* is a great choice for high school groups yet may be inappropriate for a mostly middle-aged community group. *Oliver!* requires a whole gang of young boys (or girls). You may not enjoy working with children. I believe they are a wonderful asset to any production. They add a new dimension to a show and attract audience members who might not otherwise come to your show.

ABILITIES: Consider the vocal, dance and acting requirements for the characters in each show. Is the lead a tenor? Bass? Soprano? If your strongest females are contraltos and a show calls for a soprano lead, this isn't the best choice. Do the chorus members need to be skilled dancers as in *A Chorus Line* or *Forty-Second Street* ? Is the choreography based on classical ballet as in *Oklahoma!* and *West Side Story*? Consider the libretto. Although musicals are not known for their strong scripts, many require a mature level of acting skill.

DEMANDING LEADS: Some shows are "star vehicles" and require an extremely talented lead who will appear in almost every scene such as in Eva Peron in *Evita*. One of my tensest moments as a director came during auditions for a high school summer theatre production of *The Music Man* with no Harold Hill in sight. Fortunately, we were able to recruit a theatre major from a nearby university who was thrilled to attack such a meaty role. We were lucky: he wasn't just a warm body, he was good.

PRODUCTION STAFF: The availability of people with expertise in theatre production can also dictate your choice of shows. If a show requires extensive dance, you'll need a skilled choreographer. The flying of *Peter Pan* demands a skilled technical person, and *Cats*, innovative costuming and make-up and highly stylized "cat-choreography." As a beginning director, I made the mistake of thinking I could do it all myself. I couldn't, not without sacrificing other aspects of the production.

It may be that your organization has a skilled production staff already on the payroll. Usually this is not the case. Choose a show with production requirements which match the expertise of the people in your group. Of course you can expect to attract new and talented people. However, don't pick a Bob Fosse show without a choreographer or *Hello Dolly!* without a Dolly Levi. I've never quite been able to create a silk purse out of a sow's ear. The most I ever got was an interesting handbag.

What Facilities Are Available?

The physical properties of the theatre where the performance will take place can be of great importance. Consider the size of the playing area, capacity of the house, wing-space, dressing rooms, lighting and sound capabilities, and other technical aspects of the building. Even small details can affect how you stage a show, or if you stage it at all.

The production staged for a 1500 seat auditorium is much different than that for a 300 seat theatre or a warehouse with a capacity for 100. Some musicals call for an intimate setting. Others, with large spectacle production numbers, are well-suited to a big theatre. Some shows lend themselves more readily to an arena theatre (theatre in the round) while others are best suited for proscenium staging.

Does the theatre have the lighting capabilities you need for special effects for a particular show? Are there microphones? If so, are they remote, hand-held, suspended, unidirectional, or omnidirectional? Is there an orchestra pit?

The theatre where I staged many of my shows had no orchestra pit, only eight feet of wing-space, both dressing rooms stage right, no flying capabilities and no passage of any kind from the performing area to the house except through the front curtain or out and around the entire building. I had to work around these characteristics in staging and always considered them in selecting a show. There are some things that even talent and ingenuity can't overcome.

What Shows Have Been Done Recently?

If the high school across town just staged a production of *You're a Good Man, Charlie Brown*, you likely won't choose it for your next show. If a touring company brings a production to your area, wait a year or two before staging it. Comparisons will inevitably be made and it's tough to compete with professionals. Yes, it's nice to hear someone say they enjoyed your show more than the Broadway production, but I wouldn't count on that reaction.

See the shows. Be inspired. Then, store those ideas to be brought out and used at some future date. A period of "fermentation" can only benefit. The resulting production will be yours, not merely a parody of what you've seen.

What About Accompaniment?

Almost any show benefits from a full pit orchestra, however, using the full orchestral accompaniment for a show requries a skilled conductor and musicians who will likely require payment of some kind. It would be nice if professional musicians could donate their time and expertise, unfortunately, this is rarely the case.

Most shows work fine with a "combo" accompaniment. This usually consists of keyboards, bass, guitar, and percussion with a possible added wind or brass instrument to cover special parts. Many orchestral sounds can be duplicated by electronic keyboards and synthesizers. I have also staged successful productions accompanied only by piano.

By examining the score and listening to the sound-track, you should be able to choose a show suited to the talent and resources of your group. You can stage a great show, even if the New York Philharmonic isn't available.

2 Bring in the Experts

The Production Staff

Staging a musical is a monumental task. Even the simplest productions in small schools and communities require many levels of expertise in a variety of areas. The production staff of a show can number as many as 50 or 60, although I have rarely seen that number. If your group is small and the show simple, it may be that you fulfill many of the responsibilities of the production staff yourself. I caution you about trying to do everything. You will drive yourself to exhaustion and the show will suffer.

Instead, surround yourself with experts. Choose them carefully. On the following pages, you will find a list of production staff personnel and job descriptions. Keep in mind that this is the *ideal* production staff. Your staff will likely be wearing more than one hat depending on the complexity of your show. The key is to find quality people who possess the knowledge and expertise to help you stage a successful production.

"Anything you can do, I can do better..."
Irving Berlin, **Annie Get Your Gun**

Directors and Designers

STAGE DIRECTOR: The stage director is usually the person responsible for everything that is seen and heard on stage. The artistic and spiritual leader of the production, he or she is responsible for coordinating the ideas, people, and resources of the show.

MUSICAL DIRECTOR: Responsible for all music in the show, the musical director is charged with analyzing the score, assisting in casting, rehearsing the singers, finding a rehearsal accompanist, procuring the orchestra (or whatever accompaniment will be used), finding a conductor, and assuring that the orchestra is prepared. The musical director may conduct or accompany or both. Sometimes the stage director and musical director are one and the same.

DANCE DIRECTOR/CHOREOGRAPHER: The choreographer of the show designs, teaches, and rehearses all dance numbers in the show as well as assists in casting. This person will work closely with the other directors.

ASSISTANT DIRECTOR: This person might be more aptly called a production assistant, for the responsibilities include everything from rehearsing small groups and taking notes for the director, to running errands. A good assistant director is invaluable. Choose someone who is eager to learn and willing to tackle any job for the good of the show, no matter how menial.

SET DESIGNER: The set designer designs all sets and scenery, draws plans for construction, arranges rental of scenery and coordinates the building of the set. Often this person designs the logo and aids in program design. It is necessary for the set designer to work closely with the director and other designers to insure conceptual unity.

COSTUME DESIGNER: This designer is responsible for designing and planning the costumes, providing sketches and directions for sewing and construction, renting or borrowing costumes, and supervising construction of the costumes. A good costume designer not only has expertise in sewing, but in the visual arts and design as well.

MAKE-UP DESIGNER: This person will design the make-up (including wigs and facial hair), buy the necessary supplies, instruct actors in techniques where necessary, and organize and supervise make-up application. Often, the costume designer designs and supervises make-up.

LIGHTING DESIGNER: The lighting designer designs and implements all lighting for the show including planning and writing all lighting cues and supervising the lighting crew. Lighting is often designed by the set designer.

SOUND DESIGNER: Often the lighting designer doubles as sound designer and is responsible for planning and preparing all sound effects and amplification. This includes procuring any equipment and supervising implementation.

Other Music and Dance Personnel

CONDUCTOR: The musical conductor prepares the orchestra or other accompaniment and conducts rehearsals and performances. The best conductors are not only skilled musicians but knowledgeable about musical theatre as well.

DANCE CAPTAIN: The dance captain rehearses the dance numbers and assists the choreographer during auditions and rehearsals.

REHEARSAL ACCOMPANIST: An extremely important person, the

rehearsal accompanist accompanies all rehearsals (often including dance rehearsals) in the preliminary stages of production until the orchestra takes over. In some productions, the musical director or the conductor is the rehearsal accompanist.

Business Personnel

PRODUCER: The chief coordinator of the production, the producer supervises the budget, coordinates all staff and plans the production schedule. This important person needs communication, financial, and organizational skills, and will certainly be more effective if he or she possesses knowledge of theatre arts as well.

BUSINESS MANAGER: This invaluable member of the production staff deals with all monetary aspects of the show, including financial records, ticket sales, and purchasing. Often the producer acts as the business manager.

PUBLICITY MANAGER: The publicity manager plans and executes all publicity for the show. This includes media coverage before and during the production, photos and posters, and arranging for play-bills or programs which may include selling advertisement space.

BOX OFFICE MANAGER: This manager is in charge of all ticket sales (advance and at the door) and supervises the box office staff.

Technical Personnel

TECHNICAL DIRECTOR: The technical director supervises and implements all technical aspects of a show. This includes organizing and scheduling construction and installation of sets and scenery, and lighting and sound equipment.

MASTER CARPENTER: The master carpenter is in charge of constructing all sets and scenery and supervises the construction crew.

CONSTRUCTION CREW: This crew builds the sets and props under the direction of the master carpenter, set designer and technical director.

PROPERTY PERSON: This person is in charge of borrowing, renting or building all stage properties and organizing the storage and backstage movement of props.

LIGHTING AND SOUND OPERATORS: These operators run the lighting and sound boards including spot lights during rehearsals and performances.

Backstage Personnel

STAGE MANAGER: The stage manager is an important position during casting, rehearsals, production week, and performances of a show. He or she is virtually in charge of running the show during the final rehearsals and performances. The duties include preparing the prompt book, maintaining schedules, organizing crews, coordinating all back-stage elements, and relaying all information from directors to crews and actors. This position demands organizational skills and a great deal of tact and common sense as well as knowledge of theatre arts.

ASSISTANT STAGE MANAGER: The assistant to the stage manager helps carry out his or her responsibilities.

STAGE CREW HEAD: This crew head is in charge of the backstage running crew and coordinates movement of props and scenery during rehearsals and performances.

STAGE CREW: Often called the running crew, they move props and scenery backstage as needed during rehearsals and performances.

WARDROBE PERSON: This person is responsible for all costumes backstage including storage, cleaning, and organizing of costume areas.

DRESSING ROOM ASSISTANTS: Their job is to assist cast members and help to maintain order in the dressing rooms.

House and Box Office Personnel

HOUSE MANAGER: The house manager is in charge of opening and closing the house during performances and supervising the ushers.

USHERS: Ushers assist the audience in finding their seats, pass out programs and take tickets at the door.

TICKET SELLERS: Ticket sellers sell tickets under the direction of the box office manager.

Again, it is important to point out that this is the *ideal* production staff. You will assemble your staff in accordance with the special needs and talents of your group. Caution: No matter how you organize your staff, be sure to delineate responsibilities to avoid conflict over who has control over which domain. This will also ensure that every job gets covered by someone.

Finding People with the "Right Stuff"

Anyone who has ever been involved in a theatrical production knows the time and energy it requires. The people you are looking for not only understand that, they are willing to dedicate themselves completely to their task for the show. Surround yourself with *quality* people who are willing to make a commitment.

"You gotta have heart..."
Adley and Ross, **Damn Yankees**

One of the wonderful things about directing a show is seeing this commitment evolve. Newcomers to the theatre do not understand what it takes.

Many people have volunteered their services simply because they knew I needed help. They seem to go through three phases: First, they are incredulous of the amount of time and energy expended on the show by everyone around them. Then, they become resentful of the infringement on their time. Finally, most of them get caught up in the magic. They are hooked and will be among the first in line for the next show.

Sometimes you lose them. There are many people who, for whatever reason, can not make that commitment. Later, in my conversations with them, they often tell me they know they missed out on something special. I always expect to see them again. Sometimes I do.

3 Dollar, Dollar, Who's Got the Dollar?

Budget and Finance

Musicals are expensive. Because of their complexity and scale, they can easily cost many times that of a nonmusical. However, with creative budgeting and an extensive promotional campaign, you can pay for the production *and* turn a profit. But don't fill out the deposit slip yet! First you must plan and organize the budget for your show. How you do this depends on the type of organization sponsoring the production.

School Productions

Most school-sponsored musicals are part of the Theatre Arts curriculum and are funded on a yearly basis. Funding is divided between the various productions throughout the school year by the head of the department. In some schools, many departments are involved and special funding is made available.

If producing a musical is not already a yearly event in your school, you need to create a budget that will fulfill your needs and still be acceptable to the administration. Rarely have I seen a school finance director who appreciates the budgetary requirements of producing a musical. In other words, you will be underfunded. And, since musicals usually go **over** budget, it is crucial to find other sources of funding.

Fortunately, audiences love musicals and with a good promotional campaign, you should be able to raise funds through tickets sales. A good rule of thumb: Keep ticket prices within a dollar of the price of a movie in the local theatre. Most districts also allow fundraising projects such as car washes, bake sales, white elephant sales, etc. The possibilities are limited only by your imagination.

Staging a school-sponsored musical can be very exciting. You have a captive cast, an enthusiastic audience and established purchasing power. School districts usually operate with purchase orders and often have credit at local stores. Although the head of the theatre department is usually in charge, the work load of the director can be divided among many departments. The music department provides vocal coaching and accompaniment, the art department helps with design, props, and scenery, and the shop department aids in construction. The home economics, journalism and business departments can also contribute to a musical.

This is also a great way to attract interest in the theatre department. New recruits are always welcome, even in big schools. And, in a school production, you usually have the use of rehearsal and performance facilities, access to printing equipment, and an easy advertising target—the entire student body and their families.

School musicals also have drawbacks. Inadequate funding and limited artistic freedom can shadow the production. Your choice of show and how it's staged is governed by school policy and subject to approval by the administration and school board. Also, directors are usually not compensated because staging shows is considered part of their teaching duties. Few administrators realize the enormous time and effort it takes to stage a musical. They simply see the illusion.

Community Theatre Productions

Most community theatre groups are nonprofit organizations. To obtain nonprofit status and a tax number they are subject to state and federal guidelines. This includes having articles of incorporation, a constitution, a board of directors and officers. Actual governance is usually left to the group.

Many groups have arts-minded citizens from the community on the board of directors often as a figure-head group with little governing power. The officers are theatre people and make major decisions. There may be a paid artistic director and a clerical staff or all positions may be held by volunteers. There are as many configurations as there are groups.

If you are planning to organize a community theatre group, contact your state government for guidelines and the Internal Revenue Service for information about receiving a tax number for tax-exempt status. I would also suggest doing research. Write to some existing groups. They will be happy to send you copies of their constitution and articles of incorporation. This will help you decide how to set up your group. Many groups have had to reorganize because the power structure **hindered** production rather than **helped**. If you're aware of the possibilities, you can structure your organization to serve the needs of the group and the community.

There are many attractions to forming a nonprofit theatre group: You have artistic freedom limited only by the structure of your organization and the conventions of the community. There is no fear of censorship unless the public doesn't buy tickets to the show. The directing and design staff can be paid, which may attract experienced theatre people. (You are not stuck working with the art teacher who doesn't know a drop from a mop.) Roles in the show can be played by adults *and* children. Your spending is only restricted by the amount of money you can raise. And, a school administration is not constantly evaluating your worth as an educator by the shows you produce.

It's much like owning your own business. You have complete independence. Unfortunately, with this independence comes responsibility. As an independent group, you build your own limb and then step out on it, taking full risk, financially and artistically.

Finance is the biggest problem facing young community theatre groups. Facilities: performance, rehearsal, office, and storage; equipment: lighting instruments, sound system, seating, and office furniture; salaries: business manager, clerical help, directors and designers—all must be funded in addition to production costs which can be enormous.

Every community theatre group needs a good business manager (financial wizard), an expert production staff (competence plus enthusiasm), and an innovative artistic director (a genius with a knack for creating something out of nothing). A good P.R./fund-raising person is essential also. Many groups get their financial start by soliciting charter members or patrons who contribute money. Though tax-deductible, these funds are not easy to raise.

Creating an independent theatre group requires talent, stamina, courage, enthusiasm and plain old elbow grease on the part of many people. It will take time (often years) and tremendous dedication. Artistic freedom is costly.

Compromise—A School/Community Effort

Having worked with both school and community productions, I've been able to experience the pros and cons of each. The artistic freedom of an independent organization is heady. However, constant worry about finances can hamper creative abilities.

I decided to capitalize on the positive aspects of both by coming up with a proposal for the local school district to sponsor the production of a musical by the community choir which was under the auspices of the district's Continuing Education Program.

The basic tenets of the proposal were: The district would provide rehearsal and performance facilities, aid in promotion and ticket sales, and provide printing where possible. Also, the district would run our finances through their accounting system. We had buying power through local district charge accounts and purchase orders. In addition, they agreed to front us the initial costs of the production (rent, royalties, etc.).

A zero-budget based operation, the school district was sponsoring us but they were not funding us. We were responsible for the cost of the production. These funds would be raised through ticket sales, fund-raising, and tuition. (Since, technically, this was a class, all participants paid a twenty-dollar production fee.) Yes, this is an unlikely risk for a school district to take. However, I had my foot in the door. I was already employed by the district and had had previous successes with a summer theatre arts program with a similar financial set-up. The school district trusted me to do what I said I would do. They did reap benefits. The success of the production was certainly a feather in their school/community relations cap.

This situation is not without risks and problems. My first attempt at a school-sponsored community choir production, as mentioned near the beginning of Chapter 1, resulted in censorship and cancellation of the district's involvement. However, the next year, with another show and new administration, we enjoyed success.

"You've got to pick a pocket or two..."
Lionel Bart, Oliver!

Setting Up the Budget

Setting up the budget for a musical can be like the chicken/egg syndrome. Some groups set a monetary limit for a musical and then choose a show that can be produced within it. Others, choose a musical and then construct a budget that will meet the needs of the show. Whatever method you choose, the two main considerations are expenses and receipts.

What Will the Show Cost to Produce?

Consider the following expenses:

ROYALTIES AND MUSIC RENTAL: The amount of royalty and rent for a show is determined by the company which owns the rights to the show. There is usually a refundable deposit and additional charges for extra scripts and scores. (Complete information is found in Appendix B.)

FACILITIES: This includes rental of rehearsal and performance halls, cleaning and maintenance, and alteration. (Seating and staging areas often need modification for each show.)

SETS, COSTUMES, PROPS, AND MAKE-UP: This includes cost of items to be purchased, materials for construction and all rental fees. This area will take much research and preparation by directors and designers to arrive at an accurate estimate.

ACCOMPANIMENT: Include in this area all fees for musicians, instrument rental and maintenance (tuning of pianos, etc.). Generally, the bigger the orchestra, the greater the cost.

SOUND AND LIGHTING: This depends on the adequacy of the lighting instruments and sound system in the performance hall. It may be necessary to rent spots or other equipment. If you are using full orchestral accompaniment, the existing sound system may not be adequate. If you rent sound equipment, also consider fees for technicians who operate the system.

PRINTING AND PROMOTION: Tickets, programs, posters, and mailouts are included in this area. Ad space in newspapers and magazines and other promotional campaigns such as T-shirts, buttons, bumper stickers or hiring the Goodyear blimp will cost also.

SALARIES AND FEES: Your paid staff might include directors, choreographers, designers, business manager, orchestra conductor, rehearsal accompanist, stage manager and more. This cost will be great or small depending on the policies of your organization.

MISCELLANEOUS: This area can sneak up on you if you don't plan for it. It includes phone bills, clerical supplies, film and processing, magic markers, duct tape and every item that doesn't quite fit any other category.

When constructing a budget, pad or increase every area of spending. You always spend more than you intend, for it's impossible to predict the fate of every penny in an undertaking as complex as producing a musical. And, this is one of the areas where more is better, especially in costuming and scenery. Audiences love extravagance.

Where Will the Money Come From?

Funding for a production can come from a number of sources:

TICKET SALES: The largest area of receipts in a musical is usually from ticket sales. This amount can be hard to predict. Consider the size of the cast, capacity of the house, price per ticket, number of performances and past patterns of attendance. And then, estimate (guess!) *conservatively*. Even though I'm optimistic by nature, this is one area where I hold back. (You can't foresee things like a tornado warning on opening night.) After a few years, you'll become quite accurate and it won't seem so much like Russian roulette.

DONATIONS: The amount of money raised through donations for a musical is only limited by time and the number of shoes you want to wear out by going from door to door. The task may be easier if you're a taxdeductible organization, although the tax laws seem to get tighter every year. Even in tough economic times, people can be very willing to contribute to the arts. A good P.R. person can organize a fundraising drive which can net thousands of dollars, although I advocate *conservative* projections for donations.

"*Hey, big spender . . .*"
***Dorothy Fields* , Sweet Charity**

PROGRAM ADVERTISING: Many groups sell advertising space in the play bill or programs. This, like collecting donations, is a good source of income if you're willing to expend the time and energy. Advertising is still tax-deductible and, with good planning, this ad campaign can net much needed funds.

One way to plan the campaign is to decide how much you'd like to raise, then determine the number of pages of ads in the program you need to sell to meet that figure. Then the challenge is to sell every page. The alternative method is to sell as many ads as you can and let that determine the number of pages. I like the first method because it gives me a goal to shoot for and a predetermined amount to plug into the budget. The main point is to be realistic with your estimate.

"And the money kept rolling in . . ."
Tim Rice, Evita

Other Fundraising Projects

Schools often sponsor projects to raise money for the theatre department. This can be a good source of income, but predicting the amount of profit can be difficult. How many cars will twenty people wash in four hours on any given Saturday?

Try combining fundraising with promotion. An effective way to accomplish this is to sell items with the show's name and logo on them: T-shirts, hats, buttons, bumper stickers, pens, pennants, etc. Selling these items weeks or months before opening night generates income and raises the public's awareness which ultimately sells more tickets.

PRODUCTION FEES: This area of income only pertains to special school-sponsored productions where the production is set up like a class and a tuition fee is paid. Project the enrollment and multiply by the fee to estimate the amount of income. When the cast and crew pays tuition, I try to insure they don't have to spend further for costumes, etc. Although I've never heard serious objections, in the heat of long and tedious rehearsals I can expect someone to say, "And we **PAID** to do this!" or "Have we had twenty dollars worth of fun yet?"

Here is a proposed budget for a school-sponsored community education production.

EXPENSES

rent and royalties	$ 650.00
costumes, sets, make-up	2000.00
orchestra (15 @ $50)	750.00
sound (equipment and technician)	1000.00
printing (tickets, programs, posters, T-shirts)	650.00

salaries (directors, choreographer,
stage manager, conductor, designer,
business manager, rehearsal
accompanist) 2850.00
miscellaneous 400.00

TOTAL ESTIMATED EXPENSES $8300.00

RECEIPTS

tuition (50 persons @ $20) $1000.00
donations 2500.00
ticket sales (1000 total seats for two performances
  @ $5 per ticket) 5000.00
T-shirt receipts 800.00

TOTAL ESTIMATED RECEIPTS $9300.00

After building several budgets (and exceeding them a few times), you'll acquire a knack for estimation. It is *always* better to overestimate expenses and underestimate receipts. The leaders of your organization, be it school or community theatre, will be thrilled and amazed if you make a profit. With careful financial planning, you *can*.

Although I understand the mechanics of finance, I'm not good with money. In fact, my staff usually does not allow me to touch money! Therefore, I attach myself to an expert. Not only does this save stress, it frees me to expend my energies on the many other tasks of directing.

4 Extra! Extra! Read All About It!

Promoting the Production

Because you want to perform for a full house and sell as many tickets as possible, you must vigorously promote your show. This is a whole new area of expertise and can be time consuming. This chapter contains some suggestions for your promotional campaign.

The Media Blitz

NEWSPAPERS: Every community is served by at least one newspaper and perhaps two or three. Most newspapers are more than willing to *sell* you ad space, but, if you're creative, you can get lots of coverage at no charge. Find out who the public interest editor is and make contact—in person and by phone. Start sending them press releases. Deluge them with information. You may have to literally park on their desk to get their attention. It's not that they aren't interested in your cause, but you'll have to compete with every other organization for their interest.

Don't do this haphazardly. If you want good coverage, *you* will have to plan it. I have nothing against newspaper people, however, I find they have a short attention span. If you want coverage every other week for six weeks, plan it yourself, step-by-step, article-by-article if necessary. Good publicity doesn't happen by accident. There are too many other events competing for space.

"Another op'ning, another show..."
Cole Porter, Kiss Me, Kate

20

Here are some possible story angles:

New Theatre Group Formed
Auditions Held
Rehearsals Begin
Whole Community Involved in Musical
Tony-Award-Winning Musical to Be Produced Locally
Tickets on Sale at Local Businesses
Local Girl Trains Dog to Act with Corn Chips
(actual story from summer school production of *Annie*)

If you've chosen a well-known show, capitalize on it. If the show is in the process of being made into a movie, plug that angle. If it was written by somebody who's had many hits, key into that. If you've cast children in the show, try that angle. Will it include three giraffes and a circus tent? Are you having to build a replica of the Taj Ma Hal in the local auditorium? Is Robert Redford guest-starring in the show? Is Carol Channing a distant cousin of one of the cast members? You can make a story out of anything and the more print the reader sees, the more likely he is to buy a ticket.

RADIO: Local radio stations are a great place to promote a musical. Most stations have a daily or weekly calendar of events. Get on it—as far in advance of opening night as possible. Another avenue that is very effective is the public service announcement. Thirty to sixty seconds of free coverage several times a day for a couple weeks can reach a lot of people. You can even use cast members to make the spot in some stations. Sometimes it's possible to get news coverage. Call the news room.

And, don't limit yourself to one station. You have no way of knowing who your prospective audience is. They may be rock-n-rollers, country enthusiasts, classical buffs, jazz freaks or moldy oldies. You want coast-to-coast coverage!

TELEVISION: For some reason, it's tougher to break into the television market. Air time is costly. But, with persistence and a little luck, you can gain valuable publicity. Start with phone calls and press releases. Contact the news people, the public interest department, the arts and entertainment staff. Try an unusual approach if necessary. Be creative. Your success depends on who notices you. The more visible you are, the more likely someone will deem your cause worthy of air time.

Be sure to contact all the local stations. Media people don't like to think that somebody else got in on a good story and they didn't. It may sound manipulative, but I've been known to tell one station that another is covering the show, even if this is not true. If you want to sell tickets, you have to get out the word any way you can.

Another place to try is the local cable television station which may have a channel for publicizing local events. I don't know who has time to watch that channel, but somebody may and it might sell tickets.

LOGO: Design a logo for your production. Use it on correspondence, programs, T-shirts, buttons, bumper stickers, etc. The more people who see the logo and connect it to your group and your show, the more likely they are to buy a ticket.

POSTERS: Posters are an effective and inexpensive means of advertising. Keep it simple—use the logo and specify who, what, when, where, and how much. Be sure it's colorful and big enough to be noticed. Put them everywhere.

FLYER MAILOUT: If your group is established, you may have a mailing list of people who have previously shown an interest in your productions. If not, start one. Have a guest book at the door so people can get on the list. Send them a flyer, perhaps a miniature of the poster. They will appreciate advance notice for your productions. You will incur a small cost—printing, labels, and postage, but it's worth it.

I have already mentioned T-shirts, buttons and bumper stickers. You can invent numerous other ways to publicize the show. In a recent production we tried a promotion gimmick called "Buy a Cast Member." Our goal was to raise $2500 in donations. Instead of going out and asking for money or selling ads in the program, we "sold" cast members. Each person in the cast and on the production staff had a price. The bigger the role, the higher the price. They were to go out and find somebody to buy them. Businesses or individuals who contributed had their name listed next to the cast member in the program. It was a success. We raised $3500.

Whatever methods of promotion you use, with plenty of planning and a little creativity, you can make it pay off. It is worth it to look out and see a packed house on opening night.

5 Burning the Midnight Oil

A Director's Homework

This is the stage in production I call director's homework. It includes everything that the director must do before casting and rehearsals may begin. It is the process of analyzing, and conceptualizing the show.

Sometimes this is done by a committee consisting of the book director, music director, choreographer, producer, and designers. Each analyzes the script and score. Ideas are exchanged and the needs and requirements of the show are discussed. From this input and his other own ideas, the director develops a concept for the show—the idea that will unite all facets of the production. On the following pages you will find criteria for analyzing each aspect of the show: book, music, and dance.

The Script

During the first readings of the script you will get a "feel" for the show. This instinct is essential to your concept of the show. However, it will not be until after many readings and careful analysis that a clear picture of how you will proceed in staging will develop. In your readings, consider the following:

Given Circumstances/Environment

> Where does the story take place? What geographical location, climate?

> When does the story take place? What period, date, season, time of day?

> What are the economic, political, social, religious conditions at the time?
>
> What has occurred before the curtain rises? What previous action has taken place?

This basic factual information is found in the script, and should be followed closely unless you are planning a major deviation from the author's intent.

Plot and Subplot

> Who does what to whom? Why? How?
> What are the methods and motivations
> for each character's actions?

One of the criticisms of musical theatre is that the plots are flimsy and often can be summed up in one sentence: *Can Maria get Von Trapp to open his heart to his children?* This could be said of many shows. Most contain at least one major plot and several subplots. However simple or complex, you should carefully scrutinize the script of your show. Once you get the big picture, analyze scene by scene for action and motivation. I find lists of verbs helpful, especially during rehearsals as you help your actors achieve believability in their actions. For example, *How* does Maria get Von Trapp to open his heart? She *cajoles, reasons, pleads, tricks, threatens,* etc.

Characters

> What age are the characters?
>
> How do they look?
>
> What is their attitude toward themselves? Other characters?
>
> What are their social, political and religious veiws?
>
> What changes in attitudes and views (if any) occur for each character?

Most characters in a musical go through a metamorphosis in the course of the show. This can include a shift in attitude about themselves, other characters, or a change in social, political, religious or philosophical views. This change is the crux of characterization, both for the actor and the director.

Often, the main characters are archetypical—they may seem shallow, simple and lack depth. Subplot characters can be more complex, even eccentric, and may require a different level of acting skill. An understanding of each character from your analysis will aid you in casting and in character development.

Dialogue and Lyrics

Typically, in a musical, dialogue provides explanation (exposition) and moves the plot (action), while song lyrics elaborate on some point of action or provide further characterization and insight into a character's feelings and emotions. Detailed analysis of the dialogue and lyrics will be helpful during the rehearsal period and will be of great importance when blocking or staging scenes.

Rhythm, Tempo, and Mood

These terms refer to the emotional tone of the show as well as the pace or speed of music and dialogue. When expressed in adjectives, they will be a big help in developing your concept for the show. These adjectives—often expressed in relation to the five senses, will be invaluable in communicating your ideas to the designers (Examples: TOUCH—rough, silky, icy, sticky. SMELL—pungent, cloying, sharp, sweet. TASTE—salty, bitter, etc.). They can be used to describe characters, sets, costumes—anything related to the show.

Also consider the pace of the show in the development of the plot and the resolution of its conflict. At what point in the show is the climax? Where is the most intensity? There may be points in the show which need to be slowed to stress or savor the moment. Other scenes call for speedier delivery of lines and lyrics. Pacing is critical, especially in comedy.

Philosophy, Meaning and Idea

The script will contain information from the author about the main idea or philosophy of the show. It is often expressed in the philosophical statements and beliefs of the characters or may even be stated directly in notes in the script. Whether it is found directly in the book or is inferred, this information is important and may provide just the spark of idea you need.

Of the many definitions of art, the one that most appeals to me is taking an object or idea and creating it anew, viewing it from a different perspective, through new eyes. A director of plays, then, is an artist in that he takes the ideas and philosophies of the playwright and composer and creates them anew through his eyes. To do this, you must first understand the original intent. That is why careful analysis is important to your concept of a show.

The Score

The musical director should analyze the number and nature of the musical numbers in the show to determine three very important things: Voice requirements for casting, number of rehearsals necessary, and nature of the accompaniment. Here are some points to consider:

TOTAL NUMBER OF SONGS: How many numbers in *ACT I*? *ACT II*?

SIZE OF NUMBERS: Solos, duets, trios, quartets, small group numbers, production numbers? How many production numbers? Where are they in the show? Is there a show-stopper?

VOICE REQUIREMENTS: What range requirements do the leads and supporting roles have? Soprano, alto, tenor, bass? What is the level of difficulty? Are there roles which could be "speak-sung"?

CHORUS REQUIREMENTS: Does the show call for a large or small chorus? Are the chorus parts in unison or harmony? What is the level of difficulty?

STYLE OF NUMBERS: What musical styles are the songs? Ragtime, march, waltz, ballad, patter, jazz, rock, country, Latin? Will they require special voice styles? Special instrumentation?

METER AND TEMPO: In what meters are the songs? Duple? Triple? 6/8? 7/8? 5/4? Mixed meters? What are the tempos?

MOOD OR EMOTIONAL TONE: Are the songs lyric, raucous, frantic, sad, exuberant? (Note use of adjectives.)

INSTRUMENTAL MUSIC: Of what length and difficulty is the overture and entr'acte music? Is there scene change music? "Curtain call music?"

CUES: Are there warning cues written in the score to signal conductor?

DIALOGUE: How much dialogue is there between musical numbers? (Some shows such as Webber's *Evita*, *Cats*, and *Jesus Christ Superstar*, have no dialogue.)

LYRICS: Are the lyrics expositional (explain the story) therefore making good diction imperative? How many songs for each character? Chorus numbers?

ORCHESTRATION: What accompaniment would be best suited to the show? Full pit orchestra? Combo? Piano? How many musicians are needed?

Each show will have its own musical peculiarities. Considering this criteria in your analysis should give you a clear musical picture of your show. It will also alert you to any special vocal and instrumental needs, aid in casting, and help you decide the number and nature of rehearsals necessary.

The time and effort you expend on your analysis at this stage in production could save you delays and headaches later. You'll hate having to transpose the entire orchestral score down a minor third because you didn't analyze range requirements of a character *before* casting. Transposing can be tedious, time consuming, *and* avoidable.

Choreography

The choreographer must examine the score and listen to the sound track to determine the dance requirements of the show. As director, I do my own analysis in addition to the choreographer's. This aids me in my conceptualization and helps me to communicate my ideas to the choreographer. In this analysis, you will consider some of the same criteria as for the score analysis:

NUMBER OF SONGS: How many musical numbers require dancing? In *Act I? Act II?*

SIZE OF NUMBERS: How many production numbers? Where are they in the show? In a traditional configuration for a musical, the opening number is a big number, there may be one or more partway through the first act, and the act may end with a big number. Often *Act II* opens with a production number, contains one or more, and the finale is almost always a large number. There are, of course, countless exceptions to this configuration.

How many small numbers require dance? Are there any dance solos?

STYLE OF NUMBERS: What dance styles are required? Ballet, jazz, tap, soft shoe, Latin, country, ballroom? From what period in history is each number? Are there any special choreography needs such as classical ballet or acrobatics?

ABILITY REQUIREMENTS: What level of dance ability is required by the leads and supports? Chorus?

CHORUS/DANCE TROUPE: What size chorus or dance group does the show call for? Must all chorus members dance?

MOOD OR EMOTIONAL TONE: What emotion is called for in the dance numbers? Light, lyric, smooth? Loud, wild, frenetic? (Again, use adjectives.)

"Fascinating rhythm, you've got me on the go . . ." ### Ira Gershwin, Lady, Be Good

Ideas for the choreography may come from the original production, although it's a rare school or community group that can duplicate professional choreography. In addition, inspiration will arise from your analysis and concept. It is essential that you and your choreographer communicate. I've had some memorable experiences. Usually, it was because I failed to communicate my expectations clearly. In some cases, it was because I hadn't analyzed the show well enough and didn't really know *what* I wanted. You'll know what you *don't* want when you see it! Better to figure it out before then.

6 Eenie, Meenie, Minie, Mo

Casting the Show

Casting the show is an exciting stage. After much preplanning, organization, analysis and thought, this is the first chance you'll get to work with actors. Now you can begin to meld your ideas with people.

Casting decisions are among the most important decisions you'll make during the course of the production. The success of your show rests on the performance of your cast. No amount of fancy scenery, splendid costumes or special lighting effects can cover a weak cast. And, even your great directing effort cannot save you if you have made bad choices during casting. Here are some ideas that will help you organize and conduct auditions.

Get Out the Word

No matter how many talented people are in your area, if they don't know about auditions, they won't be there and you can't cast them. I know that seems basic, but often, two weeks after auditions, somebody who would have been perfect in the show tells me they would have been there but they didn't hear about it. Frustrating.

The only way to avoid this is to get the word out. Make up a press release with all necessary information about the show and auditions. It should contain performance dates, audition times and place, casting requirements (Yes, tell them what you're looking for!), audition procedures, and suggestions about what to wear during auditions.

Tell them everything they need to know, so that even with no theatrical experience, they will feel comfortable enough to give it a try. I stress the

28

words, *open auditions*. I say, "No experience necessary. Shower singers welcome!" Unless you're an established theatre organization with a giant pool of aspiring actors, you can afford to leave no rock unturned in your search for the perfect cast.

> **"What's the buzz, tell me what's a-happening . . ."**
> **Tim Rice, Jesus Christ Superstar**

Where Should These Press Releases Go?

Everywhere. Newspapers, radio and television stations, cable television companies, service organizations, schools and churches. Church choirs are a great source of talent. If this is a high school production, you have a captive cast, if not, get out to the schools anyway. Flyers sent home with every child and a good plug in the music and theatre departments can yield a lot of talent. Better yet, enlist the help of instructors of these programs.

Don't forget the power of the public service announcement. Media people can be very supportive of the arts. And, don't stop with your community, branch out. Until recently, I hadn't advertised auditions in the surrounding communities. However, in the planning stages of *Evita* (an ambitious production for a small community), it was clear that we needed as much talent as we could find. I was amazed at the response. We gained cast members, production staff, orchestra players and audience members, many who drove as far as sixty or seventy miles to participate.

You may think this is too much trouble to go through before rehearsals have even started. It's worth it. You can't cast people unless they're there. And, even if you have people in mind for certain roles, surprises can happen. Look for them. You won't regret it. The success of your show depends on it.

Organizing the Audition

Once you've advertised the auditions you can concentrate on planning and organization. This is important. If you stay organized, the audition process will run smoothly and you can give your full attention to casting.

Where Should Auditions Be Held?

Whenever possible, I audition candidates in the theatre where the performance will take place. I can then judge their volume, projection and stage presence with regard to the size of the performing area and the house. Someone who can be heard in an ordinary-sized room may not be able to fill an eight-hundred seat auditorium.

Sometimes people are terrified of being on a big stage. They freeze and you don't get their best audition. Wherever you are, you can make it work. I have held auditions in classrooms, band halls, hallways, churches, public libraries and outdoors under a tree. The important thing is to get an accurate idea of an actor's abilities.

Who Casts the Show?

This varies from group to group and show to show, depending on the size and structure of your organization. The script director, musical director and choreographer should always be present and often the producer and designers participate as well.

I have rarely seen a group of theatrical artists agree completely on anything. Therefore, I prefer the auditor group to be as small as possible. Ultimately, it is the artistic director who makes final casting decisions.

Who Conducts the Audition?

Most auditions are conducted by the stage manager. This leaves the auditors free to listen, look and think. You won't want to be concerned with the logistics of passing out information, collecting data sheets and getting the actors on and off stage. Also, a certain amount of detachment will help you to make clear judgments about the candidates. Many times I've had to audition close friends.

Distribute an audition packet to each candidate. It contains a data sheet for information about the candidates, an audition sheet which the auditors will use to assess abilities, and a character list with descriptions and information about each role in the show.

This packet also contains information about audition procedures, a tentative rehearsal schedule, a list of production staff with telephone numbers and any other pertinent details about the production. (A sample packet is contained in Appendix C.)

I want my prospective cast to know everything possible about the show. I want them to feel at ease. Auditioning can be a terrible ordeal even for professional actors. Keep in mind, however, this is not an EQUITY production.

How Long Will Auditions Take?

Professional theatre companies take weeks, months, sometimes years to cast a show. A two-day audition works well for community theatre—day one for preliminary auditions and the second day for call-backs. It is possible that a show with a small cast could be cast in one day; I like a night to sleep on it, however.

Conducting the Audition

If you have decided who the auditors are, where and when the audition will be held, and have advertised, you are now ready to start with casting. The big question now is: What Are You Looking For? You have spent weeks reading, listening, analyzing and conceptualizing the show and will have formed ideas about what kinds of actors you desire for each role. Know what you want and look for it. But, be careful not to overlook actors who don't fit your first image.

What Comes First?

The audition for a musical is divided into three sections: singing, dancing and acting. How these sections are organized and conducted will vary depending on the nature of the show and preferences of the auditors. I prefer to hear singing first, followed by dancing. Then, during call-back auditions, I schedule more singing and dancing, followed by readings and finally more singing. Musicals are, after all, mostly music!

The Singing Audition

Ask candidates to prepare a song of their choice, two or three minutes in length. Inform them that, in the interest of saving time, you *will* cut them off after three minutes. Be sure to follow through with this. The song does not have to be from the show for this preliminary audition, and generally, I prefer that it is not. They are to provide their own sheet music for the accompanist. I usually have my whole collection of Broadway hits ready for those who come unprepared. They may also sing a cappella (unaccompanied) or to a taped accompaniment.

Some candidates may ask to sing with another person. If they wish to be considered for a lead or supporting lead, I request them to sing alone. Some truly wish to be chorus members and I usually permit them to sing together. If, upon hearing them, I judge them to be able to fulfill a larger role, I ask them to sing again, alone. Usually, they are flattered enough to overcome their initial nervousness.

What Do I Look For?

During the singing portion of the audition I'm concerned with vocal range, pitch, rhythm, tone quality, diction, projection and overall singing ability. These qualities are all listed on the audition sheet with a scoring system from one through five and space for comments.

I look for one other very important quality. It has been described by various terms including charisma, personality, charm and stage presence. I call it *star quality*. It is that special quality which compels an audience's attention. Most actors either have it or they don't. Some have a lot of it. They're the ones you want.

One rule I never break when casting: No matter how poorly the singing audition is going, I never stop a candidate until the allotted time is up. Singing alone and being judged can be so unnerving that I do whatever I can to make them feel at ease. A good director knows how to court his prospective cast, make them feel wanted. You can't afford to alienate anyone, especially in a small community. The guy with the gravelly, off-key voice might be an expert carpenter!

First Impressions

After hearing everyone sing once, take a break to compare notes with the other auditors and discuss first impressions. This will give the choreographer time to prepare the dance portion of the audition. Although it will be impossible to make any final decisions at this point, trust your gut instincts and jot down some notes on these first impressions.

The Dance Audition

While the other auditors are conferring, the choreographer and dance captain will take the group and teach them a short dance sequence. You may have to divide the group into several smaller groups as space permits. The sequence of movements may or may not be from the show, but should be similar in style and difficulty.

It is important that each prospective cast member gets a chance to run through the movements several times. This process may take a long time depending on the abilities, previous dance experience and size of the group. Some will be quick studies. Others may never get it. The choreographer will want to take note of this.

For nonprofessionals and untrained dancers, this can be the most traumatic part of the audition. Even seasoned actors and talented singers can feel ill at ease during the dance audition. I remember vividly my audition for a university production of *Grease*. After completing my singing audition with relative ease, I watched as the choreographer showed the first group of candidates a series of dance steps. Having no dance experience, and little confidence in my ability to move my body through space, much less replicate the steps I was seeing, I panicked. I walked up to the stage manager, asked him to take my name off the list and left the building.

The memory of that experience has affected the way I conduct auditions. A little patience and encouragement goes a long way toward building the confidence of the dancers. You want them to feel confident so they'll show you their best audition.

Now the dance captain takes over to lead the dancers through their routine so the choreographer can become an observer. Divide the large groups into groups of three or four so that you can clearly see each dancer. I find that any less than three makes the novices too nervous. Repeat the sequence as many times as necessary until you've assessed each dancer.

What Do I Look For?

It is important to note body type. I label candidates "Type A" for tall and thin or "Type B" for short and stocky. This is an over-simplification but it may help later as you try to fit names to faces and performances.

Consider rhythm, coordination, style, speed of learning, carriage, personality, and overall dance ability. As in the singing audition, candidates are numerically scored and comments made. Watch the groups as many times as necessary to clearly judge their abilities. Be aware that with untrained dancers, what you may be looking for is "potential." Don't panic if you don't see the dance troupe of your dreams. Remember the sow's ear/interesting handbag analogy?

"Dance—ten; looks—three..."
Edward Kleban, **A Chorus Line**

Evaluating the Preliminaries

Although this may seem like judging a book by its cover, you must make decisions based on what you have seen and heard thus far. Divide the candidates into two categories: Those you believe could handle a *lead* or *supporting lead* role (these are the people you would like to hear again) and those that fit into the *chorus* category. I sometimes ask the whole group to come back for day two of auditions. This depends on the size of the group and the nature of the show.

If your show calls for a small chorus, you may have to have a third category: People that you cannot cast in any capacity in this show. This is where the size of your community and the policies of your organization come into play. Since most of my experience is with small communities, I rarely turn people away from a show. If I can't put them on stage, I invite them to join the group in some other capacity. Usually they accept. If you must reject people, do it gently. Praise their efforts. Invite them back. Rejection is a terrible thing. Professionals know that best of all.

You can post a list or make an announcement for call-back auditions. At this point, I like to explain more about the show, and about the characteristics and ability requirements of the major roles. It's important that it be known that every role is still open (even if this is not the case). Actors will give a better audition if they think they still have a chance at the role they want.

In order to prepare for the call-back audition, candidates will need scripts and music. I usually don't send the full script and score, rather some short scenes and selected songs. If you want to hear someone read for a certain role, don't be afraid to ask. There is nothing wrong with pulling an actor aside and telling him you would like him to concentrate on a particular role.

By now you will have made some preliminary judgments. At this stage I can often predict the entire cast. However, I wouldn't recommend casting this way. First, you and the other auditors need as much data as possible to make sound decisions, and second, people who audition for a show want every chance to be seen and heard. Countless times I've had people ask, "Couldn't I have just one more chance?" Even if you can cast your show from the first impressions, they will not appreciate it.

The Call-Back Audition

The candidates will likely be more nervous the second day because more hangs in the balance. A director who is positive and enthusiastic about the potential of the group is more likely to get their best audition.

Some directors start the call-back with readings from the script. I prefer to hear singing first. You will not have to hear entire songs, although when someone dazzles you, it's hard to have them stop. Actors should sing these songs *with* the accompaniment in the proper key.

The greatest audition fiasco I have ever witnessed occurred when a candidate refused to sing with the piano. She said it "made her nervous." She said she "had a cold." She said she "couldn't do it with the piano" because she "hadn't practiced it that way." The plain fact was: The role was not in her voice range. The scene that followed was incredible. I only wish I had been casting *Who's Afraid of Virginia Woolf!*

I'm always amazed at people's image of themselves. It is not uncommon for all the females to want to be the leading lady and all the men, the hero (no matter what their age or physical traits). I've had heavy-set middle-aged women audition for the role of teenage siren and slender, youthful tenors covet big baritone roles, and an unmistakably feminine woman seek the role of a macho, hairy-chested male tango singer. Once, I had someone send a cassette tape and expect me to cast them sight unseen!

"God, I hope I get it..."
Edward Kleban, A Chorus Line

Handling the Fragile Ego

It takes an enormous effort to put yourself out there to be judged and the ego is a very fragile thing. I try to give each person a chance to sing for the role of their choice as time permits. EQUITY people will laugh at this, it's so far from the reality of professional theatre. But, again, this is not EQUITY. These people will not be paid for their efforts. They are putting themselves through this agony for the fun of it! Besides, the more material you hear them do, the better you will be able to judge their capabilities.

Remember to ask for what you want. Even if they don't see themselves as you see them, they will usually be flattered that you singled them out and more than happy to oblige. (They will have plenty of chance to be upset later, after final cast announcements!)

The Reading Audition

This part of the audition enables you to assess speaking voices and acting ability. Listen for diction, tone, projection, expression and timing. You may have the actors do a prepared reading or get right down to the business of reading from the script. As small groups of actors read various short scenes, you will begin to see how the actors act and react together. As in "star quality" there's a unique reaction that occurs between some people when they're onstage together. Although it's an elusive quality and hard to measure, you'll know it when you see it. It is the stuff that makes the difference between good scenes and great scenes.

Always ask the prospective cast if they have conflicts with the rehearsal schedule. It's important to find this out *before* you cast the show. I once cast a very talented person in a supporting lead role without checking his work schedule. He missed over half the rehearsals and I had to replace him. Had I looked on his data sheet, I wouldn't have cast him. In my excitement at finding him, I didn't check. And, in his excitement at getting the role, he didn't tell me!

Making Final Decisions

As you hear different combinations of actors during the reading you will begin to see the pieces of the casting puzzle fall into place. The process of making final casting decisions is both subjective and objective. You are evaluating specific data, but you will not be able to escape your feelings about actors, nor should you. Sometimes you'll make a decision in favor of a particular actor just because he "feels" right.

As you discuss your choices with the other directors, there may be conflicts. Trust your instincts *and* be open to the ideas of others. Your strong feelings about an actor may lead to tunnel vision about other possibilities. I've had experiences with directors who refused to budge on any directorial decision, never admitting that they could be wrong. Good directors are flexible, especially when they perceive it is for the good of the show.

One criterion to consider in casting is how well the actors take direction. This is often evidenced in their demeanor during the audition—in their interactions with the other candidates and the auditors. Were they cooperative, helpful, friendly? Did they take suggestions well?

Beware of actors who are rude, uncooperative, hostile, or argumentative during auditions, a time when they should be trying to impress you. Their behavior seldom improves when subject to the pressures of rehearsal and performance and they can ruin a production. If you are mindful of this during auditions, you can avoid much conflict and perhaps even having to replace an actor.

Making the Big Announcement

Making final casting decisions is almost as exhilarating as opening night—knowing that you have a group of talented people ready and eager to begin rehearsals. Each director has his or her own method for notifying the candidates about cast assignments. A list may be posted, telephone calls made or an announcement to the group. In any case, the news will be good for some, bad for others and you'll want to approach it as delicately as possible. No matter how amenable everyone has been up to now, some feelings are bound to be hurt.

I was casting a fifth grade production of The Wizard of Oz and, of course, every girl wanted to be Dorothy. At the reading of the cast list when asked by some little girls why they didn't get the role, I replied that it wasn't that they lacked talent, but that they weren't tall enough to be Dorothy in this production, as somebody had to play the Munchkins. I thought this was a logical and humane way of explaining my decision. Apparently, they didn't. That noon they picketed at lunch wearing posters that read: "We hate you, Miss Soeby. We hope you get fired! It's not fair, we can't help it if we're short!" Moral: Be prepared for any reaction. Feelings may be hurt no matter what you say or do.

The news will be received in the same spirit it is presented. If you are positive and enthusiastic about your cast choices, it will be difficult for people to react negatively. And, be ready for anything! Every director has a Dorothy story.

Understudies or No Understudies?

This is an area of debate among directors and may depend on the size of your group. I don't cast understudies in my school and community productions for two reasons. First, it places an unfair and unreasonable burden on the amateur actor to learn the role of another character along with his own role. Even if it is the character he is aching to play, I don't like to divide his energies. And, by the end of the rehearsal period, every person in the show is likely to know the lines, lyrics, and blocking of every character. In fact, I've often had to ask actors to refrain from mouthing the lines of fellow actors while on stage. Should you need to replace an actor, any number of persons in the show may be able to fill that spot.

During opening night of a summer school production of *The Music Man*, the unforeseen happened. At intermission, a curtain fell backstage, knocking one of the supporting leads unconscious. He was to go on in the opening scene of *Act II*. While the doctor was examining him (the only time I've ever had to ask, "Is there a doctor in the house?"), one of the chorus members piped up, "I know his lines, I'll play his part!"

We sent him on to do the scene and he did it beautifully. Fortunately, the original actor was able to resume his place onstage albeit with a bump on his head. Since that incident, I've never worried about understudies.

Helpful Hints to Auditioners

Many directors get caught up in the "them" against "us" syndrome during casting. It's as if they want to establish authority and power right from the start. This is a self-defeating attitude. In order to recruit talented, hard-working, positive people you must first gain their trust and confidence. Tell them what you expect. Give them the best possible chance to impress you. Here are some suggestions for auditioners that I borrow from Michael Shurtleff's book, *Audition*:

No actor is too loud; over half are too soft.

Audition for **everything**. Don't decide in advance you're not good for a certain role.

Personality and emotion are more important than a beautiful voice.

Be willing to take risks.

Don't be afraid of being too bizarre or "off-the-wall." We are looking for **interesting** people!

And remember: **All considerations in casting are relative.**

These suggestions plus inside information on the roles should help your prospective cast feel more confident during the auditions. If they are confident, they'll give their best audition and your job of casting will be much easier.

II. Get Set...

Today's director is the principal designer of a production. Responsible for all that is seen and heard on stage, he or she must not only rehearse the performers, but synthesize a cast of designers as well. The following chapters contain information about designing and constructing costuming, scenery, properties, make-up, lighting and sound. Use it as a planning guide for the technical aspects of your production.

7 Dressing the Part

Costuming the Show

A costume designer spends many years learning the art and craft of costuming. One chapter in a book cannot take the place of art, design, and theatre classes and many years of practical experience. This chapter will provide only a basic overview of design and construction and offer some important things to consider in costuming.

Costumes make the strongest visual statement of your show. They reflect time and place, social and economic conditions, personality of characters, and suggest mood, atmosphere and idea. They must be visually attractive *and* practical.

Ideally, the director, designer and actor should have input into costuming so that the final effect is a creation of all artists involved. This collaboration helps to ensure successful "walking scenery."

"Button up your overcoat..."
DeSylva and Brown, Follow Thru

For practical purposes, I have divided the costuming process into five stages: 1. Analysis and Research, 2. Conceptualization and Design, 3. Planning and Shopping, 4. Construction and Sewing, and 5. Alteration and Modification.

Analysis and Research

The costume designer should listen to the show's soundtrack and read the script. The first readings will be for mood, imagery and emotional tone—to get a "feel" for the show. Subsequent readings are for data. What follows is a list of things to look for in reading.

PHYSICAL ENVIRONMENT: When does the play take place? What historical period, year, season, day, time of day? What time period elapses during the show? Where does the play take place? What geographical location, country, city? In the city? In the country? Outdoors? Indoors? Analyze this data scene by scene.

CHARACTERS: How many leads, supports, chorus? Age? Physical appearance? (Not only of characters, but after casting, of the actors themselves.) Occupation? Economic and social status? Political and religious affiliations and beliefs? Emotional state? Relation to other characters? This is important because costumes can visually emphasize the importance of one character and subordinate others. How many costume changes for each character? This is usually based on passage of time, however, some shows have leads changing costume numerous times just for spectacle. Your budget will dictate.

DEGREE OF REALISM: What degree of realism is called for in the script? This may also be based on the directorial concept for the show.

PERFORMANCE PLACE: Where is the play to be staged? Large auditorium? Small? The size of the theatre will dictate the scale—how far must the costumes project information? Is it proscenium staging? Thrust? Arena? or a combination? (A complete description of types of staging is found in Chapter 9.)

BUDGET CONSIDERATIONS: How much money is allotted for costuming? How many costumes or accessories need to be purchased? Rented? Constructed? Costuming always costs more than you think it will, so plan carefully.

TIME ALLOTMENT: What is the time-frame for planning, shopping and construction? The sooner the actor is on stage moving in the costume the better.

DRESSING FACILITIES: How much dressing room space is available? Elaborate costumes take more room to store and put on than simple costumes and small space will make numerous costume changes difficult.

MOVEMENT RESTRICTIONS: What movement and dancing will each character have to perform during the show? Some of this information can be found in the script. Also consult the choreographer. Better to design the costume to accommodate special movement needs than to discover during dress rehearsal that major changes need to be made.

ACCESSORIES: What accessories—hats, purses, shoes, gloves, etc.— are needed for each character? Will they need to be constructed or can they be purchased, rented or borrowed?

It's a good idea to chart all costume information: a data sheet for each character and a poster-sized master chart for the entire cast. As you design, colors and swatches of material may be added to the chart. This will help you visualize the costume needs of the entire show.

Scheduling is very important. Set up a time-line for completion of costumes. Allow time for analysis, shopping, delivery of rentals and specially ordered items, construction and sewing, fitting, rehearsals in costume and alterations. Be realistic. Allot *extra* time.

Research

A costumer's research actually begins at birth. Every bit of visual information stored in the brain is potential costume data. Every storybook, magazine, newspaper, encyclopedia, painting, sculpture and theatrical performance can provide stimulus for costume ideas.

A trip to the library will yield books on the history of dress and magazines with illustrations and photographs with valuable information on period and style. Museums, fashion magazines, window shopping, park bench sitting—the sources are endless. Start a picture file. Keep your eyes open for any possible inspiration.

Conceptualization and Design

Costumes in a show function on two important levels: aesthetically—they need to be visually attractive—and symbolically—they must convey the ideas and philosophies of the show as they reveal factual information about the story and its characters.

A period of brainstorming will help you synthesize all factual information and ideas. During this time, continue to meet with the director, other designers and the choreographer. This open line of communication is essential. Not only can these meetings yield many ideas for your designs, they may save frustration later.

Every designer has his or her own methods of creating costume designs. Most think on paper. Doodling and sketching are ideal methods for trying out design ideas. It may take many pages of sketching to arrive at one good design for a character. Here are some important things to consider as you design:

CLARITY AND SCALE: Since an important function of costumes is to convey information, it is important that the audience can see clearly. The costumes must transmit this information visually through space. Two important words: *simplify* and *exaggerate*. What seems clear on the street does not translate well to the stage. The larger the theatre, the more vital this is.

COLOR, LINE, SHAPE AND TEXTURE: All elements of visual art, they create mood, atmosphere, and emotional tone on the stage. The identity and personality of the characters can be communicated through careful use of these elements in costuming. Also, use contrast to show the position or importance of a character in relation to other characters or his environment.

SPECTACLE: Costumes should enhance and enrich the play, not detract or distract from it. However, in a musical there is usually one or more numbers which cry out for special costuming. These are often production numbers involving the whole company. In these instances you may wish to go for as much spectacle as time and money allow.

"You're never fully dressed without a smile..."
Martin Charnin, Annie

PRACTICALITY: Throughout the design process keep in mind that the costumes must be worn by living, breathing actors who must sing and dance, sometimes under difficult circumstances. Strive for safe, strong, efficient costumes. Where possible, choose durable materials which can be washed and stored easily.

Design for unity of idea—scene by scene and throughout the show. Also consider variety and balance. Attention to these design ideas will ensure that your costumes are practical, visually effective, and have the "see-ability" and "understand-ability" necessary for a successful production.

Planning and Shopping

The implementing of your costume designs requires careful planning. You'll want to provide sewing and construction crews with detailed sketches and clear instructions. This is where good communication skills come in handy. Don't leave anything to chance. You'll be frustrated and disappointed if the finished product isn't what you wanted.

Before the construction process can begin, materials and supplies need to be purchased. This often entails bulk-ordering material and ordering unusual items. It may take several shopping trips over a period of weeks to obtain exactly what you need. If you plan ahead, you'll spend less money and save numerous trips for additional or forgotten materials.

If you are planning to buy or rent costumes or accessories, locate them in catalogues and make arrangements for payment and delivery. Allow plenty of time. My costuming philosophy is: *beg, borrow, or make* before you *rent or buy* (unless it's a special item that you can't do without). You'll be surprised at how creative you can get when money or time is an issue.

Sewing and Construction

The ideal costume workshop contains layout and cutting tables, dress forms, presses, sewing machines and an abundance of tools and supplies. However, few schools or community theatres are lucky enough to have *ideal* situations. You will probably be doling out costume construction to a variety of people to be completed at home. This is where clear sketches and instructions are invaluable and close supervision imperative. Construction of special items is best done with the designer in attendance.

In a production of *Jesus Christ Superstar* we decided to have the twelve disciples wear T-shirts touting "I'M FOR JESUS." We spent a month trying to find the right color shirt and had a local business do the printing. Unfortunately, we waited until the last minute. The day before the show the shirts were delivered. They read "I (apostrophe) AM FOR JESUS"—a grammatical fiasco. With no time to print more shirts, we had to use a magic marker to blot out the apostrophe—an inadequate solution. I hated those shirts. Though, technically, it wasn't our error, it was definitely our fault. We should have allotted more time and personally supervised the printing.

Time *is* of the essence. Try to stick to the construction schedule. Delays of a day or a week mean less rehearsal time in costume and I can't stress enough how important it is for actors to get on stage in costume as soon as possible. A dress rehearsal or two is not enough in a musical. Also, it is never too early to start rehearsing in shoes, hats, and other accessories.

I'll never forget an incident in a school production of *Tom Sawyer*. In the scene where Huckleberry Finn jumps him, Tom's wig flew off and landed in the orchestra pit. It was a disaster that could have been prevented with a few bobby pins. He'd had only one rehearsal in that wig.

Alteration and Modification

After fittings and rehearsals in costume, determine what alterations or modifications need to be made. This usually involves adjustments in size, hem-length or shape of neckline, but can sometimes mean redesigning or rebuilding an entire costume. The more carefully you plan and design your costumes, the less likely that you will have to start over.

8 The Mask That Reveals

Stage Make-up

When beginning actors (men and teenage boys in particular) ask me, "Do I really have to put that stuff on my face?" I say, "Yes!" When asked why, I may reply, "This is the theatre!" or "Because I said so!" or "Just do it!" — inadequate answers, but by this stage in production there's little time for a course in theatrical make-up. Yet, there is a need even for beginning actors to know and understand the art and techniques of stage make-up. Hopefully, this brief chapter will get you started in the right direction.

Who Designs Make-up?

Some theatre groups have make-up experts on staff who do make-up for the entire cast of a production. In most school and community productions, actors are responsible for their own make-up. Usually, one person is assigned the task of designer. This person oversees the design and application of all make-up. Often, the make-up designer spends all his energies on the leading characters and special make-up leaving the majority of the cast to fend for themselves.

> *"Put on a happy face..."*
> **Lee Adams, Bye Bye Birdie**

Why Use Make-up?

A major function of stage make-up is to aid characterization. As with costuming, make-up helps to convey to the audience a character's physical and emotional state and personality. The first step in make-up design is to analyze these character traits. Some specific character information will be found in stage directions in the script. Much of it must be inferred from the dialogue and action of the play. In your analysis, consider the following aspects:

AGE: The most obvious use of stage make-up is to convey a character's age. It would be nice if all actors cast were exactly the right age, and never got any older in the course of the play. This is rarely so. In make-up, three things must be considered: the age of the character, the *apparent* age of the character, and the *apparent* age of the actor. Example: You have a thirty-year old actress portraying a forty-year old woman, who, because she's led a tough life, needs to appear to be fifty. Or, a forty-year old actor is playing a character who, in the course of the play ages from twenty-four to seventy. Each situation presents different problems in terms of make-up.

RACE: Oriental, Hispanic, American Indian, Afro-American, African, Caucasian, etc.—each has unique physical traits. *Flower Drum Song* and *The King and I* call for Oriental actors. Other shows such as *Raisin* and *Porgy and Bess* require black actors. Each presents specific make-up problems. It is also possible through skilled use of stage make-up, for an actor of one race to portray a character of another.

HEREDITY: Such characteristics as hair color, skin tone and outstanding facial features can be very important to the audience in establishing character relationships. It's highly unlikely (probably impossible) for blonde, blue-eyed parents to produce black-haired children with brown eyes. Audiences won't believe it either. Even in a musical where reality is suspended, it's best to create the illusion of the relationships on stage.

HEALTH: The character who is a "health nut" differs in appearance from a character who is cancer-ridden, obese or malnourished. Each present unique make-up problems concerning skin pigmentation, texture, and facial contours.

ENVIRONMENT: A character who is a farmer working outdoors every day of his life would have a different skin tone and texture than a public accountant. The make-up for a wealthy society woman would certainly be different than for a woman who works in a factory. The complexion of a person from Tahiti will differ greatly from a resident of Greenland.

TEMPERAMENT: The emotional state of a character has direct influence on his appearance. Shy, nervous, bold, angry, confident, reckless, fastidious, grumpy, serene—all are personality traits which can affect physical appearance.

Historical Period and Fashion

Particular attention should be paid to the time period in which the play is set. The customs and fashions of the times are extremely important to a character's make-up especially where hair styles and facial hair are concerned. Tevye would look pretty odd beardless with a crew cut just as the male characters in *Bye Bye Birdie* would not wear "beatle cut" hairstyles.

Style is even more important in historical plays or plays based on known characters. What audience would accept Daddy Warbucks with hair or an Annie with long, straight blonde hair?

The location of the play can have an influence on make-up and hairstyles also. A style that was the rage in France might not have been popular in America at the same time.

Many actors and make-up designers keep a picture file for quick reference and inspiration. Most public libraries have books on the history of style and fashion. Magazines and encyclopedias can also be helpful. Although you may not wish to copy designs from the original Broadway production of a show, they certainly could serve as a guide for your own designs.

Make-up and Distance

Of major importance is the distance that make-up must transmit character information. In a proscenium theatre, where the audience may be hundreds of feet from the stage, make-up is designed and applied differently than in arena staging where the audience is much closer. Street make-up is rarely enough although chorus members may need less make-up than leads and supports.

Make-up can also enhance facial expressions. Of what use is a raised eye-brow if the audience can't see it? Also, application of lip color will help the audience to understand dialogue and lyrics.

"A little more mascara..."
Jerry Herman, La Cage aux Folles

The Make-up Sketch

The make-up sketch is a drawing of the character's make-up. Usually drawn with colored pencils, it includes skin colors and textures, contours, wrinkles, altered facial features, facial hair (if any) and hairstyle. It delineates exactly which make-up products will be used and how each will be applied. It is a blueprint for application.

It may take many sketches to arrive at a final design. The time spent is worth it. If done in advance, special make-up products can be ordered and time-consuming experimentation at the last minute can be avoided.

Facilities and Supplies

Ideally, the dressing rooms should have running water, mirrors, and adequate lighting for applying make-up. Space is also a factor. Because musicals have large casts, make-up often has to be applied in shifts. Be sure dressing rooms have an abundant supply of tissues, and cold cream or other make-up remover.

Veteran actors may have their own make-up kits but the majority of make-up supplies must be purchased. I recommend any of the group kits which are available from most theatrical supply houses. They contain most items necessary to conventional application and are adequate for most productions.

Be sure the kits include a variety of usable base colors (creme or cake), liner pencils, cheek colors, lip colors, powder and tools for application (brushes, sponges, etc.). You will also need crepe hair for beards, mustaches, sideburns and spirit gum for application.

If make-up calls for scars or wounds or if facial features are to be altered three-dimensionally (as opposed to using shading), you may need wax, putty, latex, etc.

Hair spray, mousse, styling cream, hairpins, curling irons and hair blowers are all necessary items for styling hair. You may need colored hair spray (grey is most common), wigs or hair pieces. If a character needs to be bald or partially bald, special supplies will be needed.

Allow time for paperwork, delivery and the building of special items such as beards. Also, it's important that actors get a chance to practice application, especially if make-up is extensive or timing is a factor.

In our production of *Evita*, the hairstylist perfected the "four-minute pompadour" which is similar to performing the *Minute Waltz* in thirty-nine seconds. Without practice, it would never have been possible.

Be sure to order enough supplies for several applications of make-up. One dress rehearsal in full make-up is usually not sufficient in a musical. The shuffling of actors through the make-up mill takes as much practice as the application. Avoid last minute changes. Opening night jitters don't need to be augmented by actors who have no idea what to do with their make-up.

Learning About Make-up

Many school theatre departments have classes in make-up which include history, design and application. Unfortunately, in community theatre, make-up is often neglected and left up to the actors who may or may not be skilled.

A mini make-up workshop is a great way to educate the cast. Several hours of instruction including actual practice in application can do wonders for a cast that is unskilled and may be apprehensive. I highly recommend Richard Corson's book *Stage Make-up*. Complete with photographs, illustrations, and diagrams, it is the most comprehensive text I've ever encountered on the subject. Your theatrical library is not complete without it.

9 A Place to Play

Sets and Scenery

It's easy enough: Get a talented and experienced set designer, find a master carpenter, assemble a crew of experienced theatrical builders and— voilà!—you have your set. Sound unfamiliar? More likely this is a do-it-yourself operation. An artist friend is the designer, your chief carpenter is a local builder with no experience in theatre and the crew is made up of friends and family of the cast. Yet, with rudimentary knowledge, and determination and practice, you *can* successfully design and build a set for your show. This chapter deals with basics.

What Is the Set Designer's Job?

Ideally, the set designer possesses visual imagination and a basic knowledge of art and design elements (line, shape, color, form, composition, etc.). He has knowledge of the technical side of designing and constructing scenery. This includes structure, limitations of materials, construction techniques, and moving and storage of scenery.

He or she also has a working knowledge of theatre from the playwright, actor, and director's points of view. A good designer can perceive the playwright's goals, understand the movement of actors on stage, and is sensitive to the ideas and concepts of the director. It is crucial that the set designer have a good working relationship with the other designers and directors.

Analyzing the Theatre

First, gather basic information about the theatre where the show will be performed. Consider the following physical aspects:

47

What Type of Stage Is It?

There are three basic theatre types: proscenium, arena and thrust. They differ in the physical arrangement of the playing area and the audience. In a proscenium theatre, the action takes place behind the invisible vertical plane formed by an arch called the proscenium arch. The audience sits opposite the playing area and views the action much like watching a movie. Many older theatres are proscenium theatres.

In an arena theatre or theatre-in-the-round, the actors and the action of the play are completely surrounded by the audience. This type of theatre provides a very intimate setting for a play but can present some unique staging problems (exits and entrances as well as blocking) and is often not practical for a production as complex as a musical. Few theatres have been built solely as arena theatres although most experimental theatres have arena capabilities.

The thrust stage combines elements of the proscenium stage with the arena stage—the audience surrounds the playing area on three sides. Most modern theatres utilize some form of thrust staging and many traditional proscenium stages have been modified to place the action closer to the audience and make staging easier.

Musicals can be successfully staged in any type of theatre. It is the physical characteristics of the theatre which will determine how you design and build the set for your show. Ask yourself the following questions as you analyze your performing space:

What is the size—width, depth and height—and shape of the playing area?

If it is a proscenium theatre, how much apron space is available? (The apron is the playing area in front of the curtain.)

Are there any permanent structures or levels (staircases, columns, balconies, etc.) to consider in staging?

How many entrances and exits are there and where are they located?

Are there curtains? If so how many and where are they located? (Many theatres have additional curtains at various depths in the playing area.)

How much wing space is there in the theatre? (Wing space is the area off-stage to the left and right of the playing area.)

Is there a system for flying scenery? (A system to raise and lower drops and other scenery.)

Are there cycloramas, scrims or drops available for use?

What pre-constructed stage pieces are available—flats, platforms, step units, ramps, door frames, columns, etc.— and how many?

How many audience seats are in the house and how are
these seats arranged?
Is the seating area raked? To what degree?
With this information you can draw an accurate, to-scale floor plan and
inventory the scenery pieces that are available. It makes no sense to rent
drops when no flying capabilities exist or build step units and platforms if you
can use existing pieces. Even if you've produced many shows in this theatre,
do a fresh inventory. Things change from year to year and show to show and
it is expensive to start from scratch.

Analyzing the Play for Set Information

The set designer should explore the script or libretto. First read for tone
and mood, then examine the show's action to determine the scenic elements
called for by the playwright. These might include entrances and exits, stairways, fireplaces, furniture pieces specifically mentioned in the script and any
other items necessary to the play's action. *Peter Pan* needs to fly, *Sweeney
Todd* requires a chute to dispose of his customers, *A Chorus Line* calls for
mirrors, and Eva Peron in *Evita* must have a balcony from which to sing
"Don't Cry for Me, Argentina."

Four Functions of the Set

A set has four main purposes: It should serve as functional space for the
action of the play, establish time and place, create mood, and be aesthetically
pleasing.

Designing for Functional Space

It is important for the designer to create a functional physical environment for the arrangement and movement of actors on stage. This job is more
difficult in a musical because of the large number of people in the cast and
the necessity for dance space. One way to accommodate a large cast is to
create different levels of acting space. This can be done with platforms, stairways, scaffolding, ramps, ladders, furniture or permanent structures such as
buildings with balconies, or mountains.

Four Basic Types of Sets

THE BOX SET: The box set consists of an arrangement of flats which
form two or three walls, usually of an interior room, where the audience
forms the imaginary fourth wall. This type of set may be impractical for productions as complex as most musicals.
THE DROP SET: Most musicals written before 1970 call for a drop set.
Drops are large flat painted pieces of scenery (usually canvas or muslin)
which form the backdrop for scenes and are lowered and raised as scenes

change. While one scene is taking place in front of one drop, the set pieces and furniture are being arranged behind it for the next scene. This facilitates quick transitions between scenes. Large numbers requiring most of the playing area are alternated with small numbers which can be played in the downstage areas. Even in the absence of drops, this arrangement of small and large scenes is referred to as a "drop set."

THE UNIT SET: The unit set is an arrangement of scene pieces—platforms, stair units, ramps, etc.—which form a basic playing area for the action of the play. As scenes change, pieces can be rearranged, often with additional units, and rolled on and off stage. This type of set is very workable for most musical productions.

THE SINGLE STATIONARY SET: Occasionally, a show is written to be staged on one, permanent structure which does not require any modification from scene to scene. The action of *H.M.S. Pinafore* all takes place on the deck of the ship, the feline antics in *Cats* occur entirely in a junkyard, and *A Chorus Line* is to be staged on the bare stage of a rehearsal hall. Designing such a set would seem to be easy, however, it takes great planning and innovation to create a playing space to accommodate all the action in a play and remain visually interesting.

Typically, scripts contain very little specific information about the set. It is helpful to know which type of set was used in the original production, although it's unlikely that you'll duplicate it. Since part of the creative challenge in theatre is to find a new way to express the old ideas, try out *your* set ideas.

Designing for Time and Place

The set helps to establish the *where* (indoor/outdoor, city/country, climate) and *when* (day/night, year, season, historical period). Consider the degree of realism called for by the playwright. In cases where the director wishes to make an artistic statement by bringing an old piece to the present or the future, consider the director's concept.

Total realism is rarely expected in a musical. After all, there is nothing realistic about people singing in the middle of a conversation. Most shows call for selective realism. This is accomplished by selecting a few elements— objects or details—which characterize a particular setting or period thereby suggesting or symbolizing. It is not necessary to recreate the Parthenon to suggest Greece—a few columns should do. The forest or outdoor scene might be created by a drop, a lone tree, or leaflike projections on a scrim.

"Gonna build a mountain . . ."
Bricusse and Newley, Stop the World, I Want to Get Off

Spend time in the local library. A wealth of visual information can be found in history books, encyclopedias and books on architecture. Like the costume designer, a set designer never stops researching. Keep your eyes open. Ideas for the set can come from anywhere.

Designing for Mood

Part of the purpose of a play, as with any work of art, is to stimulate emotion. The set designer's job is to translate ideas and emotions into visual terms. Just as the painter uses elements of art to convey meaning, so must the scene designer. Consider the following elements in your design process:

SCALE: All objects on stage need to be expanded to seem of ordinary size and to transmit visual information to the back row. The most effective and innovative use of scale I have ever seen is the set for *Cats*. Since the cats were portrayed by humans, the entire set (a junkyard) was designed and built to scale, right down to the rusty soup cans and discarded toothbrush. A masterpiece of art in itself, the out-sized junk pile created the perfect setting and completed the illusion.

DETAIL/DEGREE OF BUSINESS: In design terms, broad, unbroken surfaces, large expanses of solid color, and smooth textures tend to invoke different feelings than broken spaces, much detail and ornateness. A purist would say the one is tragic and the other comedic. I like to think of these elements in context—the meaning comes from their relationship to each other.

LINE: Consider long, straight, unbroken lines versus short, broken, multi-directional or curvy lines. What meaning is conveyed if all the major lines in the set are vertical? Horizontal? Diagonal? Which suggests stability, strength? Which tension and unrest?

SYMMETRY: The degree of symmetry or asymmetry in the set also conveys tension or absence of tension. Total asymmetry creates the most uncertainty while complete symmetry indicates rest and resolution.

COLOR: Color is perhaps the strongest conveyor of emotion in the arts. A good set designer capitalizes on the communicative, associative power of color. Consider the different meanings in the color green. One hue could indicate freshness, newness, spring, while another sickness or decay. White could symbolize purity and light, or death. The red of blood, pain; the red of a rose, beauty; and black—emptiness and evil or dignity and strength.

Color can also suggest varying degrees of heat: red—warm; blue—cool. In mixing paint, adding white tends to lighten the color emotionally, while black accomplishes the opposite. The skillfull use of contrast can make a strong statement.

Be subtle. Take care not to oversimplify. Avoid triteness. Good guys don't always have to live in a white house.

Designing for Aesthetic Value

Now, step back. Look at the big picture. If your design provides functional playing area, conveys time and place, and sets the emotional tone, you can ask: Is it visually appealing in and of itself? Is it art? If your designer is an artist he will have had this in mind during the whole process. In fact, I've had to coax my artist-friend designers down out of that artistic cloud a time or two. In set design, practicality is the name of the game. A great masterpiece isn't worth a whit if it's not a functional space for the action of the play.

Be Consistent!

Consistency is another important factor in designing the set. If you don't plan to pull the curtain at the end of the show, consider not opening with it either. If the wagon, or rolling set piece for a character's bedroom enters four times from stage right, it had better enter stage right the fifth time also. In the unrealistic world of the musical, audiences crave stability. Don't bore them, but save surprises for climactic moments of the show.

Our set for *Annie* was a giant revolving, two-story set piece with the orphanage on one side and the Warbucks' mansion on the other. The piece was *not* mechanized. Rather than have stage hands on stage for each set change, we opted to use the cast to turn the platform. When it was time to switch to the mansion, the audience saw the orphans push the orphanage out of view as around came the servants.

Even though pushing a heavy set is not in the normal job description of a butler, the audience accepted it. In fact, they loved it. In a musical, you can get away with almost anything, if you do it consistently and with confidence.

Executing the Design

After hundreds of scribbles and sketches and many hours with the script and the director, you will come to a design for a set that seems to fill the needs of the show. Test the design. Ask: Is it a functional space for the action of the play? Does it show time and place? Does it convey mood and idea? Is it visually attractive? If the answer to these questions is yes, you're ready to draw the final groundplan and get on with construction.

"One brick at a time..."
Michael Stewart, Barnum

The groundplan for the set is not only a blueprint for the designer and carpenters, it is a map for the director and the choreographer. On it they will record the movement of the actors and the action of the play. Many designers build a model—a three-dimensional replica of the set. A work of art in itself, it is accurate in scale and detail down to the color of the paint and the style of the furniture. Although models are time-consuming to build, they're a great way for the designer to communicate his ideas to the director.

Andrew Lloyd Webber spent much of his childhood staging mini-musicals on an old turntable which he converted to a tiny revolving stage. Perhaps the visual stimulation that his model stage provided sparked the creative genius that we know today.

Construction

Whether or not you build a model, detailed sketches and diagrams must be provided for the construction of the set which is usually supervised by the designer and headed up by the master carpenter. There are numerous books available on set building which explain construction techniques for building standard theatrical set pieces. I will not attempt to replace entire books in one chapter. However, do consider the following criteria in building your set:

STRENGTH AND STURDINESS: Consider the stress of actors moving and dancing on set pieces, especially platforms and ramps. There are some set pieces which may need to be reinforced for specific actions.

MOBILITY: Are the set pieces easily maneuvered on and off stage as necessary during scene changes and between performances? My favorite carpenter builds everything to hurricane-strength and I often have to remind him that the pieces also need to move.

STORABILITY: Are the set pieces able to be stored between scenes and performances? This sometimes entails constructing pieces which can be folded or assembled and disassembled quickly. Hinges and hook and eye bolts are extremely useful. If your theatre has as little wing space as mine, you will soon learn how to construct compact, hideable sets.

SAFETY: In the backstage environment where chaos is the rule rather than the exception, take great care to construct the set pieces with safety in mind. Avoid leaving sharp edges and protruding nails. This general rule of safety becomes even more important in the dark of a scene change.

Use reflective tape on the edges of platforms and stair units. During the final performance of *Evita*, Eva fell from a six-foot platform as she was descending stairs in the dark during a scene change. She had negotiated those steps successfully during numerous rehearsals and several performances. Although she was not seriously injured, the accident could have been avoided.

Using Drops as Scenery

If you decide to augment your set with the use of dropped scenery, you have two options: rent the drops, or make them. Pre-painted drops are available from a number of companies. Usually ordered through a catalogue, they work well for some productions. Allow enough time for processing paperwork and delivery. One drawback: It's tough to tell what they really look like from a small picture in the catalogue, and once they've arrived, you're stuck with them.

The other option—painting your own—will insure that you get what you want but the process is difficult, time-consuming and can be expensive. I have been involved in the painting of one full-sized drop. Sewing the canvas, mixing paint and drawing and painting the design to scale was a learning experience I don't feel compelled to repeat.

You can successfully utilize other smaller units of dropped scenery. Flats, banners and other three-dimensional pieces are fairly easy to construct and manipulate, and can add interest and spectacle to your set. Audiences love to be surprised by scenery floating down from above.

Furniture

Most musicals call for some type of furniture although it may consist mainly of cubes and other modular pieces. Whether realistic or symbolic, actors need places to act and directors need places to put actors. This is especially important with a large cast.

These pieces may be rented, borrowed, bought or constructed. Renting or borrowing is less expensive but you are responsible for the safety of the merchandise. Also, alterations are not possible. Items purchased from flea markets and garage sales are cheap and can be painted, recovered, modified, rebuilt or ruined if necessary.

Some pieces will need to be constructed. I think most designers would prefer that everything be built from scratch. This ensures their designs are not altered in any way. Others relish the challenge of weaving the mismatched pieces into the overall design concept. You will decide which works best for your show.

Rehearsing on the Set

It is *never* too soon to start rehearsing on the set, especially in a musical where dancing is a factor. Any actor who has executed intricate steps while moving up a ramp knows that it is difficult and requires as much practice as possible, if only for safety's sake.

Timing becomes a factor. How many extra bars of music does it take for an actor to climb down scaffolding? Ascend a staircase? If the cast is large, the actors may need plenty of rehearsal simply to find their position on stage in a big number. And, no believable acting can occur until the cast conquers the set's obstacle course. This requires time.

Once the set is placed on stage it may need to be moved or adjusted to accommodate the action. Check the sight lines. Can the action of the play be seen from every seat in the hall? Although this is rarely the case, designers strive to make most of the action viewable from most seats. Can areas which are supposed to be "backstage" be seen from the audience? You may need to "mask" or hide those spaces. If your set pieces do not remain stationary during the show, you'll need to "spike the set"—put tape on the floor to mark the precise spot on the stage where each set piece rests. This aids the crew in placing set pieces during changes.

Certain tasks can and should be left until production week such as the final coat of paint and the addition of trim and other details. The overall design cannot be evaluated until the actors are on the set in costume. It's much easier to repaint the trim on a table than to remake an entire costume because colors clash. Use common sense. Avoid the terror of stapling, taping, spraying, gluing and sewing one hour before curtain.

Choreographing Set Changes

To preserve the magic, changes of scenery must occur quickly and easily. (At least they need to *appear* to be quick and easy!) This takes precise planning and practice. We used a car onstage in a recent production. Since it was the only transportation of one of the cast members, we waited until the last minute to rehearse with it on stage. It was to cross upstage three times in fairly quick succession. Even though we had it on a platform with big casters, turning that much weight in so little space was one of the most bizarre things I've ever seen. It reminded me of the joke about changing a light bulb. Although we pulled it off, three extra months of practice couldn't have hurt *that* scene change!

Assemble your set crew as early as possible so that they can have time to work with the set. It is important that they understand the action of the show. Also, if they feel like they're an important part of the team, they'll perform better backstage. Shows can be ruined by slow and sloppy set changes. Audiences tend to get impatient. If you're creative, you can make the set changes as entertaining as the show.

I've heard countless references to sets during intermission. Perhaps the most unusual was a remark I overheard about the set of a touring company production of *A Chorus Line*: "I can't believe I paid twenty bucks to see a show with no set!" Audiences are more aware of sets than you think.

10 Care and Feeding of Properties

Stage Properties

Stage properties or "props" include all movable objects onstage. They are often divided into two categories: set props and hand props. Set props are decorative items or objects called for by the script or the set designer. Hand props are objects handled by the actor in the course of the action. A basket of wood sitting by a fireplace is a set prop. If it is used by an actor to carry a picnic lunch or a baby, it becomes a hand prop. Let us leave the set props to the set designer and concentrate on hand props in this chapter.

Uses of Stage Properties

Props function in many ways. They aid in the telling of the story (exposition)—telephones, dishes in a dinner scene, and swords in a fight. The instruments in *The Music Man* are a perfect example of items called for in the script and necessary to the action of the play.

Props aid in characterization. The woman clutching a handkerchief or worrying a rosary, the pipe smoker, the man nervously popping a riding quirt on his leg—all provide valuable clues to a character's personality. They may also aid in focus. If one person in a crowd is waving a book, a flag or a sword, he will attract the audience's attention. The object held high in the actor's hand is in effect creating another level.

Hand props are invaluable to stage business. "Business" is any movement or activity onstage used to intensify or heighten the emotional impact of a scene. Champagne thrown in a face, a back-bending kiss, or the guy who attempts to slug somebody and hits another character when his target ducks are all examples of stage business. Usually not specifically called for in the script, it is invented by the director or the actors.

Some stage properties have the ability to make light (matches, candles, torches, flashlights) and sound (books snapping, whips slapping, canes tapping, papers rustling). Others have inherent movement—waving flags, spinning pinwheels, fluttering scarves, quivering epees.

Often in a musical, entire numbers are staged around props. Top hats and canes, colorful banners, guns or swords, fans or flags—all are visually interesting objects which, if used with a large number of people, become even more spectacular. *Singin' in the Rain*'s famous dance scene with umbrellas, "Marion the Librarian" staged with books in *The Music Man*, the orphans in *Annie*'s "It's a Hardknock Life" with their brooms and mops, beach balls in "Sur la Plage" from *The Boyfriend*—the examples are endless.

A good director takes advantage of every opportunity to creatively use stage properties to enhance the production while not detracting from it. Even in a musical where a certain amount of spectacle is acceptable, there is a fine line between enough and too much.

Collection of Props

Make a list of all props called for in the script and add any others that you may wish to use. Usually it's the director who makes this list although actors often contribute ideas for character props. This list should also contain a detailed description of each item—its size, shape, color, style, weight, and what the prop is to be used for in the play. Since it is the property person (once called the property mistress!) who will actually procure the objects, make the description as clear as possible. Pay particular attention to historical period. If the story takes place in 1920, a Mickey Mouse telephone will *not* be acceptable.

You can buy, rent, borrow or make stage properties. The least expensive route is best unless you have unlimited funds. There are many theatrical supply houses which rent or sell props. Be sure to allow adequate time for processing and shipping. As with costumes, it is never too early to rehearse with hand props. The quicker an actor starts using his personal props, the quicker he'll get in character and items which must be manipulated onstage need to be used as soon as possible. Sword-fighting, juggling, handling a cane and riding in a wheelchair take practice.

My favorite sources for finding props are attics, junk drawers, flea markets, pawn shops and garage sales. If you give out a list to your cast, you should have no trouble procuring all but the most unusual items on the list. Invariably, some props will have to be constructed. I have had some pretty unusual props created from found items, baling wire and duct tape. A little spray paint and glue, and you're in business. It's all part of the illusion.

Props and Performance

Theoretically, the property person is in charge of props. Prop tables are set up backstage. Each actor checks his props before and after each rehearsal or performance placing them where he will need them onstage or backstage for an entrance. However, in practice, actors often forget to check props, other actors move props and the result is: Lost or broken props and my special pet peeve—props not onstage when they're needed!

I don't know what it is that makes another person's prop so much more fascinating to an actor than his own. It's as if he's compelled to touch it, move it, play with it. You'd think he'd never seen such an item before. And the phenomenon doesn't seem to be restricted to beginning actors. I've often caught veteran actors fooling around with props. I don't know what the cure is short of hiring a big mean prop person who threatens the cast with bodily harm. He could wear a T-shirt that says: "Never Touch Another Actor's Props!—or Else!"

Seriously, props are an important part of a production. They are apt to be large in number in a musical and anything you can do to facilitate their use and safe-keeping is worth the effort.

11 What Light Through Yonder Pin Spot Shines

Stage Lighting

Perhaps lighting is the most technical aspect of a theatrical production. A lighting designer needs to be part electronics expert, mechanical genius, refractory scientist and colorization specialist. He's a consummate artist as well as a technical wizard.

It is not often that you have a person with these qualifications on your staff. Your lighting designer may be the set designer, the technical director or the stage manager. The drama director may also design the lighting for a show. Or it may be taken care of by a cast member who has some knowledge of lighting. It takes years to become a lighting expert. This chapter contains the nutshell version.

What Is the Purpose of Stage Lighting?

Stage lighting is the icing on the cake. It is possible to stage a production outdoors in sunlight or indoors with conventional lighting. But, the addition of stage lighting greatly augments a theatrical production. It is the element that ties together all visual aspects of the production. Consider the following functions of lighting:

REVEAL ACTORS AND ACTION: Lighting helps to establish the time and place of the play whether indoors/outdoors, daytime/nighttime. It illuminates the actors' expressions and movements which helps to convey the meaning of the dialogue and action.

ENHANCE COSTUMES AND SCENERY: The use of colorization, varying intensities, and the interplay of light and shadow can heighten the visual impact of set and costume designs.

DEFINE ACTING AREAS: Often the set is divided into specific acting areas—the different rooms of a house for example or indoor and outdoor scenes. The use of light can help define these areas for the audience. Even though other parts of the stage are in full view, lighting helps to create the illusion.

DELINEATE SCENES: Gone are the days of curtain-pulling between every scene. Not only is it hard work and time-consuming, it puts the audience to sleep. Instead, lighting is used to show the end of one scene and the beginning of the next. If the scene changes are fast and the lighting operators on top of things, the play will progress as if by magic.

> *"Curtain up, light the lights..."*
> *Stephen Sondheim,* **Gypsy**

Designer's Analysis

The stage lighting for a show must be logically and meticulously planned. There are many factors to consider as it is but one of many interlocking aspects of the production. First examine the script for clues to lighting. These are rarely spelled out specifically with the exception of special effects, but must be inferred from the action of the play. Consult with the scenic designer. Study the floor plan, sketches, and model for the set. Talk at length with the director. Obtain as much information as possible about the lighting needs of the play.

The second step is analysis of the performance facilities. If this is your sixteenth production in this hall or if you have built the theatre and installed the equipment yourself, you know exactly what you have to work with. If you are renting the building, it's important to assess the existing equipment. Make a list of all lighting instruments, control boards, and hanging capabilities.

Now you can decide if the existing lighting equipment will meet the needs of the show. Additional instruments may have to be rented. Most major cities have good sources of theatrical lighting supplies. Another possibility is borrowing from another theatre company. Or, with a little creativity, you can make do with what you've got.

Lighting the Show

Lighting a musical can be complicated, you don't just switch on the lights at the beginning and turn them off at the final curtain. There are many factors to consider:

LIGHTING THE ACTOR: The main job of lighting is to enhance the actor and his action. A lighting designer has several choices to make. What color to use, what intensity to use, and where to position the lights. Back lighting gives a much different effect than side lighting or front lighting and light projected from the level of the stage differs from lighting from above or below. Each produces slightly different shadowing on the actors' faces.

LIGHTING THE ACTING AREAS: Each area of action on the set must be lit for good visibility. The designer must ensure that the actor is lit when he is moving as well as when he's stationary. If there are vertical levels such as stairs, platforms or ladders, take care that the actor remains lit as he moves from level to level.

"To see thee more clearly . . ."
Stephen Schwartz, **Godspell**

LIGHTING THE BACKGROUND: In order for the scenery to fulfill its function, it must be seen. Whether it is an interior set with walls, a back drop of sky, an outdoor scene, a cyclorama, or undefined space, the set must be lighted. This is an area where a designer's artistic sense can come into play. Varying the color and intensity of lighting on the set helps to create the emotional tone for the show.

SPECIAL AREAS: Sometimes special lighting is appropriate to climactic moments in a show such as a pin spot on the face of an actor as when Tevye talks to God in *Fiddler on the Roof*.

SPECIAL EFFECTS: Explosions, lightning, fire, ghosts, and strobing are all examples of special lighting effects. They should be reserved for climactic moments in the show which call for the dramatic use of light.

PROJECTED SCENERY: Scenery can be projected through the use of slides, movies or gobos. A gobo is a metal cutout used with a light to produce a patterned beam. It is possible to project a city skyline, foliage, moon and stars, etc. These images can be projected on walls, screens, cycloramas, three-dimensional set forms, the floor, or on the actors.

A special note on use of slides. Some shows call for slides as part of the playwright's concept for the show. They can be very effective. They can also be a pain in the neck. My one experience with slides (*Evita*) was extremely eye-opening. We borrowed slides from another theatre company who had previously done the show, built special projection boxes (they had to be rebuilt three times), borrowed slide projectors and dissolvers and spent hours synchronizing each image with the music and action of the show.

We thought we had it together, but we were wrong. Opening night: projector number one's bulb burned out two minutes into the show. The audience saw only half the slides. We changed the bulb. Performance number two: Projector number two's bulb went. Moral: If you want to see all slides to a show be sure to attend two or three performances! Better yet, replace the bulbs before every performance!

FOLLOW SPOTS: Follow spots are a must in a musical. In big production numbers where there's lots of action and dancing, they can help focus the audience's attention on the main singers as well as brighten up the whole scene.

Hanging the Lights

I will not attempt to give technical advice on the hanging and adjustment of lighting instruments. I do offer some practical advice: The job is back-breaking, tedious, time-consuming and requires the patience of Job. With the exception of the technical rehearsal during production week, **Do Not Attempt to Hang or Adjust Lights During a Rehearsal**. Yes, you need to see lights on live bodies on stage. Fine. Hire strangers off the street. Pay them. Whatever. But, don't make your tired, stressed, high-strung cast stand there for hours like mannequins while the lighting designer makes minute adjustments. They will mutiny. The first time you break this rule, you'll understand what I mean.

Operating the Lights

The complexity of a musical requires the lighting technicians to understand the technical aspects of the lighting boards *and* be familiar with the show. The most modern equipment in the world or the most comprehensive light cue sheets are worthless if the operators don't know the show. Many directors have had the frustrating experience of dealing with a lighting operator who wouldn't get his nose out of his cue sheet, never mind that the actors were in darkness. And, don't expect a follow spot operator to find the lead singer if he's only seen him once out of costume and he doesn't know the story line.

The lighting for your show can be an asset or a liability. If it is well planned and executed with equal parts technique, artistic vision, and common sense, it can greatly enhance the production.

12 To Mike or Not to Mike

Sound Effects and Amplification

In a musical, the term "sound" refers to amplification as well as incidental sound. This may be the most troublesome aspect of your show. Though theatrical purists scoff at the idea of using artificial voice enhancement (microphones), you may once again have to throw idealism out the window in favor of practicality. The bottom line is this: Your production will be a failure if the audience can't hear the actors over the orchestra.

Solving the Sound Problem

Whether or not you artificially amplify the production, and to what extent, depends on three things: size and acoustics of the theatre, size of the orchestra, and "projectability" of your performers. If the theatre is small, your singers strong and the accompaniment limited, you may not have to use any artificial sound. A show with a cast of inexperienced singers and a full orchestra presents a whole different problem.

Unless you are lucky enough to work in a theatre with perfect acoustics or a state-of-the-art sound system, you will have to rent or buy equipment. Consider these options:

1. stationary microphones on stands
2. microphones hung from above
3. hand-held wireless microphones
4. clip-on remote wireless microphones

63

Each system has advantages and shortcomings. Standing microphones are the most common, least expensive equipment. However, if you use stationary microphones, blocking and choreography must be staged so that the singers face forward most of the time. Whereas this may not be a problem for production numbers, it wreaks havoc with leads. It can also be visually distracting.

Suspended microphones can help to solve the problem of movement; be sure, however, to use mikes that are designed to be hung. In one production we made a disastrous attempt to solve our sound problems by using miles of cord to hang mikes from the light battens. First problem: these mikes were not designed to be hung. Second problem: because we tied the cord to the light battens, the sound system picked up a terrible buzz from the lighting instruments. We wasted a lot of time and money.

Covering the entire stage can also be a problem. There's nothing as frustrating to an audience as sound that fades in and out as performers cross the stage. A combination of mikes on stands and suspended mikes can eliminate most dead spots.

Hand-held wireless mikes are usable but always remind me of Las Vegas stage shows. In certain productions such as *Bye Bye Birdie* you can get away with it, however, I can't picture Tevye holding a microphone.

I prefer good quality clip-on wireless mikes for leads and a stage that is covered by suspended or stationary mikes (or a combination of both). It has taken me fifteen years of trial and error and "making do" to come to this conclusion. There is one obstacle: cost. You'll have to sell a lot of tickets to purchase and install a quality system in your theatre. And, this is an area where cost and quality are directly related. If a costume rips during the show, it can be ignored by the audience and repaired in the wings. If your sound system is malfunctioning or screeching with feedback, your audience may walk out. Not only will you lose them from that production, they may never set foot in your theater again.

"The sweetest sounds I'll ever hear. . ."
Richard Rodgers, No Strings

Equipment Rental

Because my local theater does not have an adequate system, we usually augment it with rented equipment. Although it's expensive, there is an advantage. Rented equipment usually comes with a rented technician who can oversee the whole operation. This includes installing the equipment, running the sound board, taking care of repairs, and dismantling the system when the show closes. This can be a great load off your shoulders during production week when so many other aspects of the production need your attention.

Establish a good working relationship with your sound technicians. You are entrusting a very important aspect of your production to him. It is imperative that he know the show. Give him a script. Be sure he reads it. Go over it with him line by line. Be sure he makes notes. Then, give him a cue sheet and require him to be at rehearsals even before the sound equipment is set up. Even if he says he's experienced, he may only have done sound for concerts and you can't afford any last minute ear-splitting experiences.

During a recent production, one of the technicians became ill and was replaced with a complete stranger who not only didn't know the show, he couldn't recognize the leading characters. Imagine how frustrating it was until he finally figured out who was wearing which remote!

Unfortunately, the number of rehearsals with the sound system is directly related to cost. Don't skimp. I rank sound ahead of costumes, make-up—even lighting. It is the most important technical aspect of your show. It can make or break the production.

There are as many methods of rehearsing a show as there are directors and a multitude of texts on the subject. However, there are problems and processes unique to directing a musical. The following chapters explore the rehearsing of a musical from first reading through opening night.

13 The Essence of Time

The Rehearsal Schedule

The most important factor in rehearsing a musical is the effective management of time. If you do not organize your rehearsal time to the minute, you will not be able to pull off this major undertaking. In addition, the cast is about to invest a great deal of time in the show (more than they can imagine if they are newcomers). They need visual representation of this time in the form of a schedule so that they may rearrange their lives accordingly. Prepare a detailed schedule *before* the first readthrough rehearsal.

Rehearsing a High School Show

The time-line for a high school musical will differ from a community theatre production. High school shows are often scheduled to coincide with units of study or grading periods. The typical school musical is rehearsed over the course of a semester during theatre classes and after school. During class time you have a captive cast, however, in the latter stages of production, 50 or 60 minutes won't be enough.

Because of this, many rehearsals must be scheduled after school, evenings and on weekends. As with any show, the larger the cast, the more problems this presents. Yes, in professional theatre, actors work their life schedules around the production. But, in a high school production, you must schedule around studying, games, concerts, work schedules, family activities and friends.

The success of your show depends on the workability of your schedule and the degree of commitment you can elicit from your students. Are they disciplined and mature enough to make a commitment which will completely disrupt their lives for several months?

Many high school theatre teachers simply do not "do" musicals. They are expensive, time-consuming and there's more than enough material— Shakespeare, Greek tragedies, contest plays and other straight drama to keep most departments busy for the whole school year. A great advocate of musicals, I believe every theatre student should have the opportunity to experience at least one musical in their high school career.

Rehearsing a Community Theatre Show

The kaleidoscope nature of a community theatre cast presents an even greater scheduling puzzle. They may range in age from 6 to 76, each with separate school schedules, work schedules and lifestyles. *All* rehearsals must be held evenings and weekends and, unless your cast is small and homogeneous, this may necessitate a 12 to 16 week rehearsal schedule.

The key to a workable schedule with community groups is frequency of rehearsals. If your group is established and you're in a larger metropolitan area where competition for roles is stiff, you may be able to start with four nights a week and weekends. This is ideal and should cut rehearsal time by weeks. But with most groups you can't expect to start with nightly rehearsals the first week. They won't be willing or able to invest that much time—at least until they are "hooked!" Start with one or two evenings a week, add weekends, and increase the frequency as production week nears.

No matter how carefully you plan the schedule, prepare for conflicts and missed rehearsals. You will get frustrated and be tempted to make ultimatums: "Anyone who misses more than two rehearsals is out of the show!" Although I've made these threats, I have yet to direct a community theatre production where I could afford to carry them out. If you ever stage a major musical in a city of less than 10,000 people, you'll understand exactly what I mean—it's a miracle to find 75 willing, able bodies much less get them all to every rehearsal. This doesn't mean you shouldn't try, but, build enough extra time into your schedule to compensate for absences.

"Let's not waste a moment . . ."
Jerry Herman, Milk and Honey

Stages of Rehearsal

There are four main stages of rehearsal to consider when preparing your schedule:
1. Learning the Show (30 percent of total rehearsal time).
2. Development Rehearsals (25 percent).
3. Integration and Sequencing (20 percent).
4. Dress and Tech Rehearsals (25 percent).

In addition, include a period of theatre games and warm-up activities especially with inexperienced casts. The following chapters contain information about each stage of rehearsal.

14 Breaking the Ice

Theatre Games and Warm-ups

It would be ideal if your cast arrived on day one of rehearsals disciplined and well-trained in acting, dancing, and singing. This is rarely the case. They differ in age, occupation and social background. They may vary in theatrical experience from professional to never having seen a play. Some will be in good physical condition, others, completely out of shape. Many will not even know each other.

As director, you are charged with transforming these individuals into a performing group—a team that works and thinks as one. This won't occur automatically. *You* must affect this change—make it happen. This is time-consuming. However, the time and effort you expend toward this end in the early stages of rehearsal will be reaped ten-fold in the quality of your production.

The Warm-up

If you were a coach, you wouldn't send your players out for a big game or a long practice without warming up. So is it with a theatrical production, especially a musical. The cast needs to be prepared vocally, physically, mentally, and spiritually for the task.

These activities have many benefits. They limber and promote expressive use of the voice and body, focus attention and concentration, stimulate imagination, energize the group and develop trust. The following exercises come from many sources. Some are borrowed from fellow directors and texts on directing and others I have invented or modified through years working with inexperienced casts. Like a recipe, you can alter them to suit your directing style and the nature of your cast.

68

"Getting to know you . . ."
Oscar Hammerstein II, **The King and I**

Physical Warm-ups

Relaxation

THE YAWN: From a sitting, standing or lying-down position, relax the neck, throat, and drop the jaw into a yawn. Although we yawn spontaneously many times during a day, it may be difficult for some to produce a yawn at will. Try closing your eyes and rotating the head loosely on the neck. If this doesn't help, have the director or another cast member massage the neck and shoulders and try it again.

THE RAG DOLL: Stand, feet slightly apart, arms at sides. Let the weight of the head carry it forward, relaxing the neck and shoulders. Continue to droop forward relaxing the back one vertebrate at a time. Let the weight of the arms carry the body lower until it is hanging forward loosely like a rag doll. Help the beginners by leading them through each movement in a quiet, soothing voice. Walk around the group to find out who needs extra help. A light touch on the back and shoulders will encourage the reluctant.

THE DEAD MAN: Lie flat on the floor with eyes closed. Gradually relax the body starting with the toes and working upward through the feet, ankles, calves, knees, thighs, hips, stomach, chest, shoulders, upper arms, forearms, hands, fingers, neck, base of the skull to the crown of the head. Vocalize this quietly for the group. Have them visualize each body part as they relax it, or picture slowly swirling colors infusing the body inch by inch.

Breathing Exercises

SLEEP BREATHING: For many people, breathing correctly from the diaphragm seems difficult. They don't realize they already know how, for in sleep, the body automatically breathes from the diaphragm. Lie on the floor and relax. Breathe naturally and concentrate on how the body breathes. Try stacking books on the stomach and watch the books move with each breath. During intake of breath, the rib cage is expanding and the books should rise.

NAVEL NOSE: Another way to help insure correct breathing is to stand relaxed, feet slightly apart, with arms at sides. Now, imagine that your navel is your nose. "Inhale" through your navel. The rib cage expands. In correct diaphragm breathing, shoulders should not rise when you draw in breath.

RAG DOLL: During the rag doll relaxation exercise, breathe in. If you are breathing correctly, you will feel your back and rib cage expand upward.

LEAKY TIRE: Breathe in deeply, expanding the rib cage. Now, hiss like a leaky tire as you exhale. Feel the pressure on your diaphragm muscle.

EXPLOSIVE "H":   Breathe in deeply, expanding the rib cage. With your hand on your stomach just below the rib cage, exhale in short bursts saying "huh, huh, huh" with an explosive beginning "h" sound. You should be able to feel the contraction of the diaphragm muscle with each burst of air. Work with a partner. Put your hand on your partner's stomach to check for correct breathing.

Stretching and Limbering

THE RUBBER BAND MAN: As you lie on the floor in a relaxed state with eyes closed and arms and legs extended, make believe your body is a rubber band. You are now being pulled by an invisible force. First, your right hand and left foot are being stretched in opposite directions, then your left hand and your right foot. Now, your arms are being stretched apart, both feet against your arms, your head away from your body, etc.

SLOW MO: A leader stands in front of the group or inside the circle and moves in slow motion as the group mimics each movement. Isolate arms, legs, head and feet first, then, progress to whole body movements. (Dance captain or choreographer may lead this exercise or have cast members take turns as rehearsals progress.)

UNDERWATER WALK: Imagine that you are standing underwater. Feel the weight of the water on the body, on your hands, arms, and legs. Now move through the water. Reach for an object, carry something heavy, try to reach the surface.

Strengthening and Energizing

DANCE TILL YOU DROP: Dance captain or choreographer leads group through a series of short repeated rhythmic dance movements to music with a strong, fast beat. (Music does not have to be from the show. Any high-energy dance music will suffice.) Since you are trying to build endurance, style doesn't count. Start simple, arms first with clapping or snapping combinations. Then add legs. Keep the sequences short to ensure success by even the least accomplished dancer in the group. The leader changes movement when entire group can execute the series. Continue this activity until the group is winded. Increase time as endurance builds.

Vocal Warm-ups

Limbering the Vocal Chords

THE SIGH: Sigh as if you were tired. Now, using that same relaxed sigh, start on a higher pitch and let the voice fall lower until it is a mere relaxed vibration.

THE SIREN: Using a "whoo" sound, swoop the voice up and down like a siren. Don't worry about specific pitch. Gradually increase the range swooping up a little higher each time before swooping back down. This should feel relaxed, not forced. Use a hand movement to indicate direction. It is a great way to increase a singer's range. Novice singers sometimes have a mental block about high notes and learning to siren may release some of that vocal tension.

THE HUM: Humming is an excellent way to warm up vocal chords. Starting in a comfortable range for singers, hum a descending five-note scale. Start a half-step higher for each repetition. Use a piano for accompaniment so singers can easily find the pitch. Be sure everyone is humming correctly with lips closed over open teeth. Humming properly produces a tingly vibrating sensation in the lips. If it tickles, they're doing it right.

Vowels and Consonants

DESCENDING VOWELS: Starting in a comfortable range for the singers, sing the syllable "*aw*," in a descending five-note scale. Raise a half-step for each repetition. (Using "*aw*" instead of "*ah*" will produce a more pleasing in-tune sound.) Change the syllable to "*oh*" and then to "*ooh*." Never force the sound. Strive for relaxed, resonant, in-tune singing.

UP AND DOWN VOWELS: In a comfortable range, sing "*aw*" upward five steps then downward (*do, re, mi, fa, sol, fa, mi, re, do*). Raise a half-step each repetition. Change it to "*Mee-oh-mee-oh-mee-oh-mee-oh-mee*," then, "*may-oh-may . . .*" or "*migh-oh-migh*," etc.

"The rain in Spain . . ."
Alan Jay Lerner, My Fair Lady

EXPLODING CONSONANTS: Say "*Puh, puh, puh . . .*" spitting out each consonant. Then, "*tuh, tuh, tuh,*" and "*buh,*" "*fuh,*" etc. Check for correct breathing from the diaphragm. Be sure to explode the sounds. Overdo it. I usually say, "If you're not spitting on the person in front of you, you're not trying hard enough!"

TONGUE TWISTERS: Practice crisp consonants and enunciating words by saying and singing tongue twisters. Start with the familiar, "Peter Piper." Speak it clearly, increasing tempo with each repetition. Then put it to music.

Another lesser known but effective rhyme is "The Tutor":

> A tutor who tooted a flute
> Once tutored two tooters to toot.
> Said the two to the tutor,
> "Is it easier to toot or
> to tutor two tooters to toot?"

ALLITERATION NONSENSE: Make up a sentence of complete nonsense using like consonants such as "*Mommy made me mash my M and M's,*"

"Donny dunked his donut in the dish," "Perry parked his Porsche in the park," or invent a phrase from the dialogue or lyrics of the show. Now sing the sentences using the ascending and descending five-note scale pattern. For variation, have some fun with expressive singing by using different emotions for each repetition: "be frustrated, envious, joyful, insane, angry, tired, proud, elated," etc. encouraging gestures and movement for emphasis. Some directors may cringe at this artificial imposing of emotions, however, remember the nature of the group. Your cast likely contains non-actors or people whose only singing experience has been in a formal choral setting. Since in the theatre, everything must be bigger than life to be seen from the back row, their real life experience may not be enough. I've even directed veteran actors who, though brilliant in straight drama, have difficulty delivering a song. Whatever you can invent to help them is worth it, no matter how contrived.

Voice Projection

Beginning actors often speak with a squeaky, breathy voice that is not audible from the second row. And, when the director insists they project, they yell the lines. This results in LOUD, squeaky, breathy voices which still aren't audible or understandable. Projection has very little to do with volume. If an actor finds the most resonant level of pitch for his speaking voice, focuses the voice forward into the "mask" of the face, uses appropriate vowels and crisp consonants, and manifests a high energy level, *he will be heard.*

RESONANCE: Finding the most resonant level of pitch for the voice can only be accomplished by experimenting. In your normal speaking voice, say a short phrase such as "I will find my voice." Repeat the phrase using a slightly higher pitch each time. Think of your head as the sound box of a musical instrument and place your voice forward in the face. You may have to go up and down over the same pitch range several times until you can feel the vibration in your cheeks and nasal passages. If your face tingles, you've found it.

If you are speaking in your proper resonance range it will seem effortless—there will be no tension in the vocal chords. Of course, the real test is if you can be heard. If you've been using a speaking voice that is too high or too low, correcting the problem will take practice. Find another cast member to monitor your voice during rehearsals.

How does this translate to singing? Hopefully the director has matched song range to singers during the casting process. However, if each song were written entirely in the narrow resonance range for each singer, the songs would be extremely boring. In addition, composers seem to think the more notes they pack into the song, the better. Therefore, the singer must be especially careful to use good vowels, clear, crisp consonants, and a high energy level to project those notes in the song that are too high or low. It's a mind over matter situation and is where the phrase "selling the song" is most apropos.

And, *very important*: Directors and choreographers should be very careful not to further hamper projection by requiring actors to do double somersaults while delivering the song!

Sound-Movement Exercises

SOUND ECHO: The leader invents a sound such as "*yeeow,*" "*beep,*" "*myrakkk*" or "*zzzoweeeyahh.*" Any sound will do, the odder, the better. Group echoes the sound, trying to duplicate the pitch, volume and intensity of the leader. Increase speed. Don't think. React!

Now, add a movement for each sound using the whole body. Twirl, kick, swing, jump, shake—spontaneous, large, free movements. This gets the cast doing two things at once and forces them to lose themselves in the experience. Encourage speed and spontaneity.

Once they've mastered echoing a sound and movement, send it around the circle. Leader invents a sound/movement and sends it to the person next to him. Receiver mimics the sound/movement then invents a new one and sends it on.

THE MACHINE: Standing in a circle, the leader makes up a "mechanical" sound and a movement to go with it which physically connects him in some way to the person next to him. As he continues to repeat his sound/movement, the next person adds a new one to the "machine." Continue adding machine parts until the whole group is involved.

Concentration Exercises

THE MIRROR: This exercise can be done to slow, soothing music, or in complete silence. Stand with a partner. One person is the leader, the other, his mirror image. The leader moves hands, head, torso, etc., as his image mirrors his movements. Use the whole body, reaching the stretching through each movement. Partners look into each others' eyes and should not speak. Switch leaders. Switch partners. Vary the activity by using music with a faster, more definite beat.

Now, try this exercise using everyday situations—shaving, putting on make-up, dressing, brushing teeth, doing the dishes. This is, in effect, mirrored pantomime.

GROUP MIRROR: Put four people in a group, a lead couple and an image couple. Choose an activity such as a barber cutting hair, a dentist working on a patient's teeth, a singles tennis match, a couple eating in a restaurant, etc. Whatever the lead couple does, the image couple mimics.

Try this with bigger groups and choose situations such as watching a movie, playing volleyball or basketball, chatting at a cocktail party—the possibilities are endless. In group mirror activities, every person in the image group has a target person in the lead group to mirror.

In the early rehearsals of *Evita* we experimented with group mirror activities of actual scenes from the show. I chose cast members to mirror each movement of characters in the scene. It was a great opportunity to see themselves in action through the activities of their "mirror." It was good for concentration, focusing energy and we had a lot of fun with it.

Improvisation

A period of improvisation and theatre games can make the difference between a good show and a spectacular show. It is an experimenting, learning, trying-on time where anything goes and all things are possible. In improvisation all cast members can succeed and all can learn from and play off of each other.

These activities help develop characterization, physicalization, relationship, stage business, emotional awareness, spontaneity, concentration and can enrich every other aspect of the performance. They are especially helpful in teaching inexperienced actors to find the objective and meaning in a scene. Consider this time not as a luxury but as an essential ingredient in the "glue" which holds your cast together.

You can find thousands of theatre games and improvisation exercises in theatre texts or invent your own. Here are a few of my favorites.

Object Exercises

Each action on stage must be justified to be believable. Very early in the rehearsal process you can help the cast see how important objectives are. Divide the cast into two large groups. Have one group sit in the audience and the other group on stage. Give the group on stage no instructions other than "I want you to stand on stage." Then have them stand there for five full minutes while the others sit and watch. It is not long before you see foot shuffling, giggling, and other awkward, nervous movements. They may try to interact with each other, the other group or ask questions like "What are we doing?" or "How long do we have to do this?" Show no mercy. Simply repeat the request that they stand on stage.

Seasoned actors may guess the game and be able to stand still without manifesting symptoms of nervousness but even they may have trouble. This is because they have no reason for being there—they have no clear objective.

Now put the other group on stage while the first group watches. Give them a specific instruction such as "I want you to count the seats in the first twenty rows," or "I want you to stand and read silently the first seven pages in your script." There is no shuffling, no nervousness. They have something to do. They have a clear objective, something to concentrate on. Let the two groups discuss their experience. You may want to let each group experience *both* situations. This is a great lesson.

Object exercises aid actors in clarifying objectives in a scene. Each action on stage must be justified. What does the character want and what do they do to get what they want? Help the actor express these objectives by asking themselves questions, "What do I want?" and "How do I get it?" Then express the objectives in first person, "I want you to _____." Now express the "how" using verbs. "How do I get what I want? (I beg, plead, cajole, threaten, bargain, etc.")

Two-Person Object Exercises

THE SANDWICH: Person One is sitting on a park bench eating a sandwich. His objective is to enjoy his sandwich in peace. Person Two comes along and is starving, hasn't eaten in days. His objective is to get Person One to give him the sandwich. (The sandwich-eater might express his objective: I want you to give me the sandwich. Then he might beg, bargain, trick, threaten, etc., to get what he wants.)

THE SWEATER: Two sisters are in their bedroom. Sister One has a new sweater she hasn't worn. Sister Two has a date and wants to borrow the sweater. Objective for Sister One: To get her homework done. Sister Two's objective: To borrow the new sweater.

THE CAR KEYS: Two persons, father and son. Father is reading the paper. Son's objective: To get Father to lend him the keys to the car for a date. Father's objective: To read his paper in peace and not let him have the keys.

Other suggestions: Returning an item to a store, ordering from a waiter, riding in a taxi. Or choose a situation from the show and let the characters improvise. Expand the object exercises to include three or more people. Examples of situations: A family eating dinner, driving in a car, or shopping in a store.

The more experienced your cast becomes at this activity, the more complex you can make the situations. It is great fun to do large group improvisations—situations such as eating at a restaurant with several tables of diners, waiters, the maitre d', manager, etc., or being at the movies with a packed theatre. If everyone has a clear objective and sticks to it these activities will be successful and beneficial. Otherwise, they may turn into a meaningless free-for-all.

Character Exercises

THE INTERVIEW: For this activity, you will need good-sized pictures or photographs of people from different cultures or occupations depicting them in situations—one person in each picture. You need at least as many pictures as cast members. Spread the pictures out on the floor or pin them to a bulletin board. Each cast member chooses a picture of the same gender that appeals to him. (Give no other clues about the activity at this time.)

Now, give them five minutes to create a character—to make up a story about the person in the picture. This should include name, occupation, age, place of residence, family history, etc., the richer in detail, the better. When the time is up, arbitrarily put them in groups of two and instruct them: "This is your favorite talk show. You are now the person in the picture. Your partner will be the talk show host and interview you. Then you will switch roles." This activity takes time but it will stimulate imagination and get the cast "thinking on their feet."

THE INTRODUCTION: This is a great activity for the very first session together. Everyone needs a partner, preferably someone they don't know well. Have them spend five minutes getting to know their partner. Instructions: "In five minutes you will introduce your partner and tell us three facts about him. One of these facts will actually be a lie and we will have to decide which facts are truth and which one is the untruth. Be sure to let your partner know what you are going to say so they don't give you away."

Trust Exercises

It's a long journey from casting to opening night and it's important that your cast members have a good working relationship. Like a winning team, the most successful performing groups function like a well-oiled machine. They not only work well together physically, they are spiritually connected. Here are some good activities which can help to develop that trusting relationship.

HAND MASSAGE: Some people may be reluctant at first to trust their body to another, especially a stranger, however, a hand massage should be fairly non-threatening. Get a partner, take his hand and instruct him to close his eyes and relax. Firmly massage the palm, fingers, and back of the hand. No tickling. If you are using too much pressure, your partner will tell you. Take your time. Switch hands. Change places. Switch partners. The first time, this activity may be done with a leader quietly guiding step-by-step through the massage.

SHOULDER MASSAGE: It takes a little more trust to allow another person to touch your torso but massage is now so accepted that the cast should think this is a great treat. This may be done with the "massagee" lying on his stomach while the "massager" sits on the small of his back or with both persons seated on the floor. Use firm continuous movements and be sure to massage muscle, not bone. Switch positions. Switch partners.

For variation, have the group sit in a circle, all facing the same direction (right or left). Now each one massages the shoulders of the person in front of him so that the entire group is connected in a circle of massage. This is a great closing activity after a long grueling rehearsal.

"Consider yourself at home..."
Lionel Bart, Oliver!

BLIND MAN: Done with a partner, one person is the "blind man," the other, the leader. The blind man closes his eyes and lets his partner guide him around the room. Try negotiating stairs and other obstacles. Be extremely careful. Now change roles. Remember the "do unto others. . ." rule!

For variation, guide your partner with words only, not holding on to him. You'll be surprised how this will hone communication skills.

These are only a few of the exercises and activities which could be used. Do not attempt to try them all in one session! Choose one or two from each group, repeating them occassionally. Important Note: The key to the success of these activities is whole-group participation. Warming up is not a spectator sport. Everyone in the room should participate—including the director. Setting the correct tone for an activity is as important as the activity itself. Your cast will not follow you into battle unless you are willing to put yourself on the line with them. You will not lose authority, you will gain respect as someone who is willing to get right in there and show them.

A few weeks into rehearsal you may be tempted to skip these activities because they are time-consuming and opening night looms imminent. Don't. It is time well spent. I admit I didn't always believe in the importance of these preliminary activities. I was always reluctant to relinquish precious rehearsal time. My views on the subject were changed for me by a situation over which I had no control. Due to a shipping mix-up the music for *Evita* was four weeks late! I had a cast of seventy waiting with bated breath to begin the task. And so I seized the opportunity and we played and experimented, improvised and invented, created and explored.

It may have been the most profitable time we spent together. I know it allowed us to make the gigantic leap from "adequate" to "wonderful" and may have been the singular reason we were able to accomplish the fantastic feat of producing *Evita* at all.

15 Take It from the Top!

Learning the Show

No matter how popular the show, it's unlikely that the whole cast will be familiar with it. The first rehearsal should be a complete readthrough of the libretto and the score by the entire cast so they begin to see the "big picture" and how their characters fit into it. Cast members read lines and the musical director plays through the songs from the score. (Actors may or may not sing along as the directors prefer.) This may be a good time to listen to a recording of the show.

This rehearsal is exploratory—it is a get-acquainted period. Spend extra time on theatre games and warm-up activities. It's also a good time for directors to talk about their philosophies and expectations for the show. If the show is long, this readthrough may take two rehearsals.

Teaching the Music

Teaching notes and lyrics should be the first priority in rehearsing the show. Music is the single most important aspect of a musical and no other progress can be made until this is accomplished. In many groups, only a few cast members read music, therefore, music must be taught by rote. This is a time-consuming process. The keys to accomplishing this are frequency and repetition. In the first stages, work on the music at every rehearsal, singing each song several, if not many, times.

Production Numbers First

Start with production numbers. Typically, chorus members have the least experience and need more time to learn. Also, these songs, because of sheer numbers of people, are more difficult to stage. The sooner the cast knows the music, the sooner they can start to learn the choreography.

"Let's start at the very beginning . . ."
Oscar Hammerstein II, The Sound of Music

Learn the Notes

A good technique for learning notes is to sing *"doo"* or *"lah"* instead of words. (This can also be effective later when the cast knows the words and you are trying to get them to communicate the emotion behind the lyrics.)

If the score calls for harmony, decide which chorus members will sing it and teach those notes right from the start. Novice singers tend to gravitate to the melody so it is important to instill the harmony into their memory from day one. If, after much practice, the singing still sounds muddy and the harmony seems to detract from rather than add to the song, you may have to eliminate it and put everyone on melody. But, don't be too hasty with this decision. It is easy to eliminate the harmony in later stages of rehearsal but impossible to put it back in!

Breathing and Phrasing

As you rehearse the music, introduce proper phrasing based on the musical line and structure of the lyrics and remind the cast about breathing from the diaphragm. At this stage, do not ask for volume. Your first goal should be proper production of sound, on pitch, with a pleasing tone. There will be plenty of time later to say, "I can't hear you!"

Enunciation

This is a pet peeve of mine. Singers who are classically trained make the most beautiful open vowel sounds but often you can't understand a single word. No matter how pretty the voices, if the audience doesn't understand the lyrics you're lost. Stress consonants. Speak the lyrics as if they were lines. Put some space between the words. Use the punctuation. *And,* discuss the meaning. Remember, lyrics communicate information. In a well-written musical, the songs are functional as well as entertaining.

Memorization

The key to memorization is repetition. Drill, drill, drill. Sing each song several times in succession. If necessary repeat short sections. Stress key words, use symbols, pictures, word associations—whatever it takes—until all notes and words are learned. There are those who advocate letting the cast "absorb" their lines and lyrics as a natural product of rehearsal. This will not work in a big musical! You have too many layers of frosting to put on this cake. Don't risk leaving out the eggs! It is terribly difficult to put them in *after* the cake is baked.

Blocking the Show

In a musical, blocking includes all un-choreographed movement of actors and falls under the responsibility of the book director. There are two basic kinds of blocking: directed blocking (preplanned movement dictated by the director) and organic blocking (movement which "evolves" naturally out of the play's dramatic action during the course of rehearsal).

Directed blocking is most often used in a musical for practical reasons. It takes less rehearsal time because the planning is done by the director *before* rehearsals. Also, if you have inexperienced cast members, they are not likely to *feel* anything except self-conscious if you ask them to invent their own movements.

One of my first acting experiences was a disaster because the director chose to organically block the show. She kept saying, "Just do what feels right on that line." I was a novice. Nothing felt right and I had no idea where to move. I wanted to be "directed" by that director! I quit the show. That terrifying experience taught me a lot about directing inexperienced actors.

Preplanning Blocking

Plan the blocking *before* rehearsals begin. Charting the movement of the actors on paper will help you explore the possibilities and visualize the movements. Sometimes called "paper blocking," this is another time-consuming but necessary part of a director's job. It will also save precious rehearsal time. It is inconsiderate and wasteful to keep the cast sitting idle while you dream up each move during a rehearsal.

The Groundplan

The groundplan is a scaled-down drawing of your acting area and set. Usually prepared by the set designer, it should indicate entrances, exits, walls, platforms, stairways, doorways, furniture and any other information about the playing area. When pasted in the prompt book opposite each page of script, you can easily use it to record blocking.

Use small triangles, squares, or circles to represent each character in the scene. Show movement by drawing lines with arrows to indicate direction. Use a different colored pencil for each character. In big scenes use simple x's and o's or numbers to show crowd position.

Paper blocking takes practice. At first you may find it difficult to visualize live actors in a three-dimensional space. You may find yourself manipulating small objects or asking complete strangers, "Would you mind just standing here for a moment?" I used to sit in a restaurant and move silverware, glasses, and salt and pepper shakers all over the table. I got some strange looks from waiters and other diners, but it worked. You will develop a system that works for you.

Designing the Blocking

Composition (sometimes referred to as picturization) is the arrangement of actors on stage. Like a still photograph of the action of the play, it is the "picture" that is presented to the audience. The director, like an artist, "composes" this picture.

Body Position

Many factors influence composition. One consideration is the position of the actor's body. If he is facing the audience, we say he is in the *"full-front"* position: his back to the audience—*"back"*; facing right—*"profile"* and so on. Like the points on a compass, there are eight basic body positions. (See Fig. 1.)

These positions take on special meaning when two or more actors are on stage. Consider the different emotional connotations of two characters facing each other in full profile, back to back, or both in profile facing left (Fig. 2).

In positioning your actors, keep in mind that an audience comes to a play to *see* and *hear*. Since most people "hear" by reading lips, you don't want to place the actors in full-back position very often except to convey special meaning. There are no strict rules, but let common sense be your guide.

Acting Areas: Depth and Width

The stage can be divided into various acting areas. In theatre terms an actor standing near the front of the stage—closest to the audience—is said to be standing *"down stage."* If he's at the back of the playing area we say he is *"up."* This comes from the period in drama when the stage was actually on an incline slanted toward the audience. Today's theatre usually has a level stage and raked seating.

The playing area can also be divided horizontally so that an actor can be *right, left or center* stage (from the actor's standpoint). Figure 3 shows the stage divided into ten playing areas including the apron.

Certain areas are said to be "stronger" than others. For instance, an actor standing alone *down center* usually commands more attention than an actor *up right* mainly because the *down center* actor is closer to the audience. Also, in western civilization where we read left to right, the *down right* acting area (to the audience's left) is stronger than the *down left* area.

Levels: Vertical Position

The other consideration in placement of actors on stage is vertical position—the level of the body, especially the head. An actor can be standing, sitting, crouching, kneeling or lying on the stage. You can extend the vertical possibilities by placing actors on platforms, balconies, stairs, furniture and other set pieces. (See Figs. 4 and 5.)

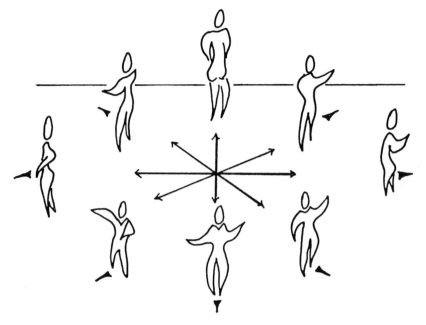

Figure 1: Eight Body Positions

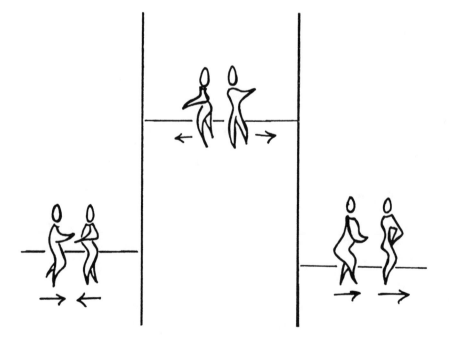

Figure 2: Relative Body Positions

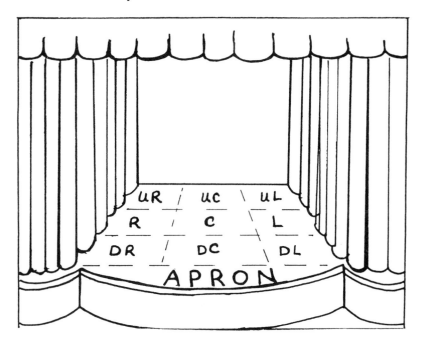

Figure 3: Ten Acting Areas

Creating Meaning in Composition

When two or more actors share the stage, it is their position *relative* to each other that is most important. Consider the meaning conveyed by a lone actor sitting in a chair *down right* in a full front position while two other actors are *up left* facing each other in one-quarter profile. (See Fig. 6.)

Now, take the same three actors. Put one actor *down center* in the chair and the other two kneeling at his feet with their backs to the audience (Fig. 7). There are hundreds of variations when you consider acting areas, levels, and body positions. Each combination can help you visually convey meaning and relationship.

Focus: Creating Emphasis

Just as an artist creates focus in his painting with the use of line, shape, and color, the director can create focus to show the relative importance of a character in a scene. There are many ways to accomplish this. Focus can be created by using the eyes. If all actors on stage are looking at a particular character, the audience's attention will focus there also. Body position can create focus when all actors on stage are turned toward another character. Even stronger emphasis is created when these characters use arm gestures toward the character or point with a hand prop—a pencil, book, hat, handkerchief, cane, etc. (See Fig. 8).

Fig. 4: Vertical Levels

Fig. 5: Vertical Levels
Using Set Pieces

Figure 6: Body Position and Vertical Levels Establish Relationship

Figure 7: Body Position and Levels Establish Relationship

Figure 8: Using Arm Gestures and Props to Create Focus

You can use space to create focus by contrasting the horizontal positions and depth of actors. If a group of actors is *down right* with a lone character *up left*, the audience will focus on the lone *up left* character (Fig 9). Similarly, if you place one character *down center*, and all others *up* of him, the *dc* actor will draw the focus (Fig. 10).

Varying the vertical positions — levels — of the actors is another effective way to focus attention and create emphasis. If one actor is on a platform and the others are on the floor, it is obvious which will seem more important. If you place the lone actor on the floor in a reclining position with the others standing, the reclining actor will draw the focus (Figs. 11 and 12).

Climactic Compositions

The distance between characters conveys relationship and meaning also. Two actors are in a "climactic" composition when they are within six feet of each other. This usually indicates extreme love or hate. A general rule: save climactic compositions for the climactic moments in the show. If you use them too often, they lose impact.

Movement

There are only two kinds of movement on stage: Movement *toward* another character or object and movement *away*. It is how far, how fast, what route, and in what manner the movement takes place which conveys the meaning. The key to successful blocking is using *appropriate movement*.

Figure 9: Using Space, Levels, and Relative Position to Create Focus

Figure 10: Creating Emphasis with Space and Relative Position

Figure 11: Use of Vertical Position to Create Focus

Figure 12: Use of Vertical Position to Create Focus

Every movement on stage needs a reason—a motivation—to be believable. There are some exceptions to this. In a scene with forty people on stage, crosses or entrances and exits may have to be staged for purely logistical reasons. The audience usually accepts this in a musical where reality is suspended anyway.

Motivation

Motivation for movement comes from two sources: Movements dictated by the playwright to get a character to the place of the action, or motivation from the dramatic action. The latter is found by analyzing the dialogue. If an actor is pleading for something from another actor, he might advance toward that actor. The other actor might back away or try to escape. If the "escaper" gets frustrated by the "pleader," he might advance toward him in anger which would send the "pleader" in retreat. It is the varying combinations of advancement and retreat—this cat and mouse game—which make movement on stage visually interesting. And, if the movements are logically motivated, they will be believable.

If it is necessary for an actor to get to a certain area of the stage and no obvious motivation can be found, you may have to invent a reason for the cross. Perhaps there's a bowl of fruit there or he has left his coat. Getting into position for a song often has to be purely arbitrary and is commonly accomplished by vamping (repeating) a few bars of music as the characters get into place.

Distance, Tempo and Route

The distance an actor travels and the speed of the movement help to convey meaning. Generally, the longer the distance, the stronger (more important) the cross. A faster cross is stronger than a slower movement. In blocking, take your cues from real life but remember to exaggerate all movement for the stage. In order to be understood by an audience, every movement must be bigger than life.

A good groundplan has physical "obstacles" which the players must navigate around to get from one acting area to another. They create tension in the movement toward and away from other characters. In a musical, arranging this obstacle course can be difficult because open space is needed for dancing. This is where a good set designer is essential.

Adjusting the Blocking

As you design the blocking for your show, you will find hundreds of combinations which convey the desired meaning. Exploring these possibilities on paper will help you visualize; however, if you find that all your paper plans don't work with live bodies on stage, don't be afraid to make adjustments. A major musical production is a complex layering of ideas and actions in the visual recreation of a playwright's dream. Experimentation is necessary to the creation of art.

Teaching the Blocking

The blocking rehearsal is conducted with scripts in hand. Every actor should carry a pencil during rehearsals. Pencils rather than pens because rented scripts must be free of marks when they are returned to the company. As you give each character his moves, he should immediately record them in his script.

Beginning actors will need to be shown the best way to record these movements in the script. Do not assume they know about abbreviations, etc. Using *d* for *down, u for* up, c for *center, x* for *cross* will help when it is time to read blocking and lines simultaneously.

At this stage it is not necessary to say lines unless you are experimenting with emphasis. Movement BEFORE a line emphasizes the line and movement AFTER a line emphasizes the movement. Most often the line and the movement are done together saving the special emphasis for important lines or movements.

After the actors have marked the blocking in their scripts, have them walk through each scene. At this point you may or may not be able to tell if the pre-planned blocking works. If it doesn't work you can fix it on the spot. If the solution is not obvious you may want to wait until further into the rehearsal process. The problem may solve itself. If the actors sense that a movement seems awkward they may "organically" find a better solution. If not, you can experiment later.

Choreographing the Show

Inventing the choreography for a musical is one of my favorite tasks. My personal dance experience is limited, yet, I've been successfully choreographing shows for years. There are a number of things which have enabled me to do this:

> 1. Ability to accurately visualize space and the movement of people on stage.
>
> 2. Understanding all the possibilities. (This comes from seeing many shows and looking from a choreographer's perspective.)
>
> 3. Knowledge of music and dance styles—historical and cultural as well as theatrical choreography.
>
> 4. Ability to correctly assess the skill level of the dancers in the cast.

5. Willingness to seek technical and stylistic advice from professional dancers.

6. Ability to quickly and clearly teach dance movements to non-dancers.

Whether you do it yourself, or call in a professional dance person, it takes a great deal of planning. As with blocking, most of this should be done before rehearsals begin. Many important decisions need to be made before you can set your ideas down on paper. The music and dance analysis (see Director's Homework, beginning of Chapter 5) will provide important information. Here are some additional things to consider in choreographing:

SIZE OF NUMBERS: Exactly how many persons in each number? Principals? Secondary characters? Chorus? If the director says, "I want every cast member in this number." The dance possibilities are quite different than for seven or eight dancers.

Are there any "show-stoppers"—big extravagant numbers whose main function is to stop the action and celebrate the moment with great music and razzle dazzle?

COSTUME CONSIDERATIONS: Will any characters be wearing special costumes or footwear which could hamper movement? This came up in *The Wizard of Oz* with the Tin Man. Even though his costume was light, he continually lost his balance, fell and could not get up without assistance. It was too late to rebuild the costume so we made do by having the Scarecrow help him up. This made for interesting choreography! If we'd planned ahead, we could have avoided the problem.

DANCING SPACE: In production numbers space is a primary issue. How much space is available? Are there set pieces—platforms, ramps, stairways, furniture, etc.—which can be utilized for movement? There are some classic examples of ingenious use of the set for choreography. The fire escapes in *West Side Story*, the junk yard in *Cats*, and the table-dancing scenes in *Man of La Mancha* and *Oliver!* are only a few. With a large cast you need to find new ways to utilize space effectively.

SKILL LEVEL: Do the dancers have to sing and dance simultaneously? What is the skill level of each cast member? This may be the most important consideration. Yes, have high expectations *and*, be cognizant of the abilities of your cast. Be realistic.

A situation came up in *Annie* where the servants at the Warbucks' mansion were much better dancers than they were singers. The choreographer was thrilled at their level of competency and invented a wild and wonderful tap number without regard to the fact that they had to sing also.

The music was complex and involved harmony. They simply could not execute both difficult tasks together. Not only were the actors frustrated, this created conflict between the musical director and the choreographer. Of course, the choreographer did not want to water down the dancing and the musical director couldn't wave a magic wand over the singers. It never was fully resolved and, as a result, it was the weakest scene in the show. Realistic expectations and better communication could have prevented the problem.

Preplanning the Choreography

The dances are so numerous and so complex in a musical, that choreography should be preplanned on paper or, at the very least, in the mind of the choreographer. The tight time schedule of a musical does not warrant a choreographer creating the dances, movement by movement, off the top of his head. If your choreographer insists on working this way, be sure to plan for extra rehearsals. Better yet, find a better organized choreographer!

Choreographing on paper takes skill and practice. One of the big challenges is the accurate visualization of space. Consider that one normal-sized adult standing on stage will occupy approximately four square feet of space even if he doesn't move! Now, put twenty or thirty twirling, sliding, kicking people on stage in a production number and you realize that if you don't have a good sense of space, you'll end up with Keystone Cops or worse!

Don't be afraid to waste paper. It is not unusual to go through 50 or 60 copies of the groundplan to invent the movements for each number. The final plan for a production number may take seven or eight pages. As with blocking, use circles, triangles, x's, o's, numbers and arrows to denote people and movement. Use colored pencils to signify groups or individuals. The final product is likely to resemble a "quarterback sneak." The main thing is: Can you decipher it later when it's time to stage the number?

Creating the Dance

The key to great choreography is visual variety and contrast. As you invent the movements for musical numbers, large or small, consider these things:

LEVELS: As in blocking, choreography will be more interesting visually if you make good use of levels, using the body and the set. Take every opportunity to use tables, chairs, stairs and any other object on stage. One of my favorite scenes is the classic move in the "Good Morning" number from *Singin' in the Rain* where they tip the sofa as they dance over, on and around the furniture. The same show contains the famous tap number on desktop and chairs.

If you're directing a show that has no levels built into the set such as *A Chorus Line*, your use of body levels is even more crucial. Remember that dancers do not have to stand straight and tall all the time. They can execute moves from a reclining position to lifting each other high into the air. Utilize all the possibilities.

BODY POSITION: Unless it is a song where each syllable of lyrics must be understood, all bodies on stage don't need to face full-front during a dance number. And in the big instrumental interludes you can point your dancers anyway you wish including backwards and upside-down!

CONTRARY MOTION: Find ways to vary the movement. Groups or individuals can counter each other moving in contrasting or opposite directions—left/right, up/down, high/low. That way, when the whole company moves in unison, it will be doubly effective.

VARY SHAPES: In choreographing large groups in a dance number, use a variety of lines and shapes—circles, triangles and blocks as you group characters on stage for movement. Use many different lines (straight, diagonal, curvy, v's and inverted v's) and vary your groupings. It is impossible not to duplicate configurations but, be cognizant of all the possibilities.

SYMMETRY/ASYMMETRY: Whether you use symmetrical or asymmetrical compositions in your choreography will depend on your set and on the director's concept for the show. Remember that symmetry generally gives a feeling of rest and resolution and asymmetry, tension and conflict. Also, consider that your audience may be visually bored by too much symmetry, so save it for special moments.

STAGE BUSINESS: Musical numbers are a great place to include stage business especially in numbers where a principal character is interacting with the crowd. A classic example of this is Harold Hill's antics during "Trouble" in *The Music Man*. The more physical activity—movement, gesture and pantomime—you can pack into a big crowd scene, the better. I love a show that I have to see several times to catch everything.

Remember, every chorus member doesn't have to use the same gesture. Encourage them to experiment with various movements to express emotion until they come up with one that works. Then, be sure they do it the same way each time. If they have trouble, invent a movement for them.

HAND PROPS: Do not miss the opportunity to add color and spectacle by using props to enhance a number. The top hats in *A Chorus Line*, parasols in *Hello Dolly!*, beach balls in *The Boyfriend*, brooms in *Annie*, books in *The Music Man*, swords in *The Pirates of Penzance,* and umbrellas in *Singin' in the Rain* are all ingenious examples of using hand props to spice up a production number. And, in many cases, they became the trademark for the show.

Teaching the Choreography

A good choreographer has the ability to teach the dance steps to the cast quickly and in clear, precise, understandable terms. I confess that I don't know an *arabesque* from a *pas de bourée,* but the plain fact is: neither do most of my cast members! So, when I say "skip-hop with a slide" we understand each other perfectly.

Always teach dance steps separately from lyrics and notes. Use the sound track or piano for accompaniment. I have found that tape decks with variable speed control make learning much easier. If you are going to use the sound track, make sure the dancers understand that live accompaniment will sound different. Unless you've hired the Boston Pops, the change is always quite a shock. But, don't let this deter you from using the sound track. The energy level of the recording will be infectious even at the rehearsal stage.

Production Numbers First

As with music, teach the big numbers first. I like to use a chalk board. No, I've never been a sports coach (!) but, my years of experience in the classroom have taught me to consider the different learning styles of my students. Some people comprehend much easier if you draw them a picture, while others learn by verbal instructions or showing them. It is best to use a combination of all three.

Label the groups in a dance number (*Group I, II* or *Red Team, Blue Team*) and divide complicated numbers into sections. It is not unusual for me to show the group "*Position A,*" "*Position B,*" "*Position C,*" etc., and then show them how to get from one position to another. I have no idea how Bob Fosse or Michael Kidd teach their choreography, but, *this method does work!*

When you have the basic positions and steps learned you can add details and work on arm positions, style, etc. I've had some success with showing video tapes of the show or dance sequences in the same style. Utilize whatever will teach and inspire your cast.

"Won't you Charleston with me . . ."
Sandy Wilson, **The Boyfriend**

Another helpful tool is the video camera. Just as most people are surprised at the sound of their voice on tape, they are often not aware of how they look when they move. You may be constantly reminding them to keep their head up or extend their arms and they may be sure they are doing it. However, seeing visual evidence is often more effective. It is especially beneficial when working with body tension and energy level. Those limp noodles who don't believe it when you *tell* them, may change into live wires when they *see* themselves.

There are some cast members who still can't bring their energy level up to the rest of the group. They are afraid to be noticed. I've often wondered why these people participate. It's as if they are attracted to the very activities which scare them the most. In these cases I teach *Lesson Number 452:* The audience will focus on the one person who is doing something *different* than the group.

This can be illustrated quite effectively with a simple demonstration.

Have a group of ten people stand on stage. Whisper to nine of them the following instruction: "Look out into the audience and point to the exit sign *Stage Left* with your left arm." To the tenth person whisper: "Look at your right shoe and keep your arms at your side." Yes, this is a bit contrived, but, if your fearful cast member is watching, it will be obvious, even to him which person draws the focus. Then the trick is to get him to *apply* his new knowledge.

Smaller Numbers: Duets and Solos

Don't expect the small musical numbers to take care of themselves. They need as much planning and attention as production numbers. The only difference is that principals and small groups can probably do much of the practice without you or the choreographer in attendance. And, experienced actors may be able to add to and augment the dance steps you already have planned. Be sure to periodically "check up on" the progress of these numbers or you may find that their creativity has gotten completely out of hand or gone in a direction opposite your concept for the number.

Proper Shoes

A word about footwear: Dancers should rehearse in the shoes they will wear for the performance (or a reasonable facsimile). If a number is to be performed in army boots with taps, waiting until dress rehearsal to feel the weight of those boots is not a good idea. At the very least they should wear appropriate dance shoes for safety's sake. (No street shoes.) Sneakers are acceptable, but, I generally encourage cast members to invest in proper shoes.

16 Layer by Layer

The Development Stage

Before development rehearsals begin, the cast should know all lyrics, lines, choreography and blocking. Where the learning stage was concerned with putting together the skeleton of the show, the development stage is adding meat and muscle. It is an exploratory period when all aspects of the show will be examined in detail to determine what actions and emotions best serve the show.

Book Development

During this segment of rehearsal the book director concentrates on developing characterization, relationships, adjusting blocking and adding stage business to the show. It is this work on the details of the show which will make the difference between an "amateur" production and a hit.

Developing Characterization

The first step in characterization is analysis. Each actor should analyse his character with respect to the following criteria:

> age, physical characteristics
> social and economic status
> religious, political, and philosophical beliefs
> emotional state
> relationship to other characters

This informaton is found in the script. If it isn't directly stated, it can usually be inferred from the dialogue and actions of the character. (A sample characterization worksheet can be found in the Audition Packet in Appendix C.)

The next step is to analyze the dramatic action of the play. Each actor should examine dialogue and lyrics in each scene asking himself these questions:

> What do I want?
>
> How do I get what I want?
>
> How do I feel about this person?

Now, he finds verbs for each line of dialogue which can easily be translated into action (cowers, shames, provokes, ridicules, begs, rejects, etc.). Encourage actors to write down their analysis and add to it as rehearsals progress.

Characterization for the Chorus

In most musicals the chorus members are simply described as "people of River City," "patrons of the tavern," or "friends and relatives." In some shows, it may be necessary for cast members to be in several different groups—a difficult task for inexperienced actors.

I believe a character work is as important for chorus members as for leads. It adds emotional depth and believability to the group. In addition, chorus members often feel that their role isn't as important as the other more prominent characters. Work on character development adds to their feeling of worth in the production and gives them something concrete to focus on.

You may wonder how they can do a character analysis with so little description and little or no dialogue to analyze. Very simply: They *invent* their character! Give them basic information and your ideas about the group. Then turn them loose to come up with a character with a name, background, beliefs and emotions. You'll be amazed at their inventiveness. It will thrust them securely into their roles and give the crowd scenes much more depth and meaning.

Adding Stage Business

Stage business is defined as "minor physical action by the performer." This can include movement, gestures, actions involving props, and facial expressions. Every show contains business. It is the interesting, often humerous, activity which helps to explain the action of the plot or reveal a character's personality.

Usually not given in the script, most stage business is invented by the director or the actor out of the action of the play. In a musical, the director will sometimes add business just for its entertainment value. Take care that it doesn't detract or distract from the necessary focus of a scene.

A typical example of stage business in *Oliver!* is Fagin's actions during "You've Got to Pick a Pocket or Two" where he demonstrates to Oliver how to pick a pocket. He's aided in this by the other boys and a variety of hand props—handkerchiefs, jewels, wallets, etc. It adds visual variety and humor to the scene as well as illustrates the lyrics of the song.

Adjusting Blocking

It is during the development stage when lines and movement are learned that you will be able to determine whether or not your paper blocking really works. Actors will be more comfortable moving and speaking and you can begin to see if the movement seems natural and believable. Take time to experiment, but be careful of making too many changes.

I am notorious for changing my mind (a woman's prerogative not withstanding!) in my quest for the perfect visual composition. This frustrates my cast. They don't understand that I'm trying to create a masterpiece! They only know that I've changed the blocking six times. It reminds me of Kirk Douglas painting the Sistine Chapel in *The Agony and the Ecstacy*: "When will you make an end?" he's asked again and again by the Pope. His reply: "When I'm finished!" Sooner or later you have to say that the scene is finished and be content with it.

Developing the Music

During this period the musical director should continue to have separate music rehearsals. With notes and lyrics learned, the emphasis will now be on phrasing, style, enunciation, projection and adding emotional emphasis and meaning to the music. Experiment with gestures. It is not enough that the music sounds pretty—it must *look* and *feel* good also. In fact, at this point, I encourage my singers to deviate from *pretty* and strive for *real*. I continually say, "Make me believe you!," "I don't understand the words!," or "I can't hear you!"

Chorus members, inexperienced as they may be, can always give more than they think they can. They can always be louder, clearer, more sincere, crisper, fuller and have more energy. Do not allow them to consider themselves less talented or less important than the leading characters. The chorus sets the tone for the entire production. A wise director recognizes this and woos them from casting until the final curtain falls.

For the principal characters, the development rehearsals are especially intense. Finding the emotions, meaning and motivations in each song and then executing them while performing vocal (and physical) gymnastics, is no easy job.

Wise use of your time and space is necessary here because you have many small scenes and musical numbers to work on. You may want to send two characters who have a scene together into a corner to experiment as you work with others. I once relegated the priests in *Jesus Christ Superstar* to the bathroom to work on their scene. I don't know what they did in there, but it worked!

Developing the Choreography

The choreography will take longer to learn than the book and music. At this stage, continue separate dance rehearsals. Drill and more drill—these rehearsals will be long and exhaustive. If extra rehearsals are necessary, schedule them. Cast members may grumble, but don't think for a minute that they want to appear on stage unprepared. I often find that their expectations for themselves are even higher than my expectations for them.

The sooner the steps are learned, the sooner the choreographer can concentrate on style, grace, energy, emotion and personality. It is not enough that the dancers be in step (although I have often felt lucky just to get them that far!), the dances must begin to have life and meaning in the context of the show.

Development and Creativity

The development stage of rehearsal is perhaps the most creative time for the director. You will have already explored hundreds of ideas in your analysis and conceptualization of the show, but, it is now that you get to test these ideas by actively manipulating people on stage. It's a stimulating, exciting time. If you use this time wisely and creatively, you will find that the other stages of rehearsal fall neatly into place and your show will have great depth and feeling.

17 Putting It All Together

Integration and Sequencing

By now all music, lyrics, dance steps, dialogue and blocking have been learned. You have dissected each scene carefully to find the emotions and motivations which work and have added stage business where appropriate. Work on characterization is progressing. You have "set" the blocking after a period of experimentation to find out what works. You are able to go through musical numbers, dance sequences and short dialogue segments without stopping to fix big problems. You have pasted, cut and painted the hundreds of small pieces to the puzzle. You are now ready to put it all together.

Scene Integration

The first step is scene integration—taking the three basic components of a scene (vocals, dance, and dialogue) and fitting them together. Up to now, you may have rehearsed a big dance number without singing the lyrics and you have rehearsed the musical numbers separately from the dialogue. The actors know their individual parts but don't know how it all fits together.

"We go together..."
Jacobs and Casey, Grease

The biggest challenge during this segment of rehearsal is the transition from one segment of a scene to another. How does an actor get from the dialogue part of the scene into the big production number? Do chorus members exit after the number or remain onstage until the end of the scene? No matter how carefully you have preplanned the entire production, when you get to this stage, logistical problems will arise which you'll have to solve on the spot.

At this stage the director functions much like a traffic cop at a busy intersection—directing the entrances, exits and movement of all the characters in each scene. In a musical, this is no easy task and, some decisions must be made arbitrarily. If an actor has to come on *stage right* in the next scene, he logically needs to exit *stage right* in the previous scene. If this seems unnatural, you may have to invent a reason for him to do so.

If he has a costume change during the scene or between scenes you must take that into consideration. Where possible, it's best to have all of a character's costume changes take place in the same dressing room. This will enable him to keep his costumes corraled in one place. (For some characters this is many costumes with dozens of separate pieces.) Unless the dressing rooms are centrally located, this means staging most of his exits and entrances from the same side. If it takes five minutes to reach the dressing rooms, quick changes need to be made in the wings.

Even though you won't be in costume at this stage, it's not too early to *talk through* and then *walk through* changes for timing and to get used to where the changes come in each scene.

Scene by Scene

Deal with each scene separately during the integration period with no special regard to the sequential order of scenes or acts. I start with the most complex scenes first. They require the most time because of their length and because of sheer numbers of people in the scene. I concentrate on each scene until I feel the cast has a working idea of the logistics and then go on to another scene. When all scenes in the show have received this treatment I make a chart to assess how far along each scene is in this process. My categories read something like this: 1. "No Earthly Idea," 2. "Somewhere in the Ballpark," 3. "Hanging Together," 4. "In there!"

From this chart I can easily see which scenes need the most work. The object is to get every scene into the last category. Then you're ready to put them in order.

Sequencing the Scenes

Now, for the first time, you are ready to work on large segments of the show in performance order. This is an exciting time in production. After weeks of focusing on detail and hours of drill and repetition, this is the first time the cast will get to see how it all fits together. Tired feet, weary minds, and lagging spirits will be revived and the cast will have a new sense of direction for they can now see more clearly the vision that you as director had when you decided to do the show.

"One foot, other foot . . ."
Oscar Hammerstein II, Allegro

When you begin to sequence the show, budget your time wisely. If you spend all your time on *Act I* and skimp on *Act II* your show will be lop-sided. I read somewhere that second and third acts in musicals "tend to take care of themselves." Baloney! The second act of most musicals already has enough problems because often all the good musical numbers are in *Act I*. In addition, the climax of the show, both emotionally and musically, is in *Act II* and will need special attention. And, your audience will remember the last thing they saw and heard (*Act II*!). You want it well-rehearsed and memorable in a *positive* way.

Start with *Act I, Scene 1* and proceed from there. Again transitions and traffic management will be the biggest problem. Solve those problems as they arise taking care not to make major changes unless absolutely necessary. (If you have planned well, you won't need to make many changes.) Each act of a musical is about an hour long. This makes it impossible to work with entire acts at once. Divide each act into several manageable sections. Once you've sequenced the sections and solved all the transition problems, you're ready to rehearse an entire act.

The first time you get all the way through *Act I*, expect a lot of cheering. The cast will be elated and proud as well they should be after putting in so much effort. You and the other directors will, of course, be able to see hundreds of flaws. This is not a good time to expound upon them! Take time to savor the moment but, don't waste too much time celebrating. The ballgame is far from over. There's much work ahead and you need to stay on track.

When you can run each act separately without major complications, you are ready for the first complete runthrough of the show. Conduct this rehearsal without stopping. This will be the most frustrating rehearsal of the entire production because you will be able to see many places where work is needed and adjustments required. And that is precisely what this rehearsal is for: To assess the status of the production on many levels.

Take notes and have the other directors do so also. Can you understand the dialogue and lyrics? Are the dances working? Do they need to be restaged or just polished? Does the stage business work for each scene? Are all cast members in character? Are your compositions and picturizations visually effective? How long is the show? Do any scenes drag?

The most important question to be answered from this first runthrough is: Will you need additional rehearsals? Whole cast rehearsals? Chorus rehearsals? Dance rehearsals? Principal rehearsals? In my experience with amateur casts, it is most often the dance sequences which need extra time, especially if the dancers must also sing. At this stage with two or three weeks until opening night, you have time to schedule extra rehearsals for whichever group needs it.

If you have used the learning and development rehearsal time wisely, this stage should be relatively painless and the show should come together without major problems. I have been involved with productions where this was not the case. The show was not ready and we had to postpone opening. With practice, you will be able to accurately assess the progress. It may be that an extra rehearsal or two will be enough to salvage the show.

18 Icing the Cake

Runthrough, Tech and Dress Rehearsals

Congratulations! You've had the first runthrough of a complicated, multifaceted musical production and it's hanging together. You have a show! That's the *good* news. *And*, as you step back and assess the show, you are verging on panic because you see a million details to fix, and opening night is two weeks away. How, will you ever fix it all by then? The answer is: step-by-step.

Everything from now on is simply icing, detail, polishing—and, as with the previous months of work—effective time management is the key.

Runthrough Rehearsals

By now, you are rehearsing on the set with all platforms, ramps, stairs, door units, furniture and all other set pieces completed. Details, painting, trim, etc., won't be finished but all parts of the set are functional and the set crew is performing scene changes.

You are using all hand and set props for business and musical numbers. Leads and supporting leads are rehearsing in some costumes, especially those which involve negotiating difficult movements such as descending stairs in a long gown. The lighting crew has light on the set. It may not be finalized, colorized, etc., but you are rehearsing with stage lighting. (And, perhaps more importantly, the lighting operators are getting to know the show.) Now it's time to perfect and refine the show. Important note: **Never conduct a runthrough rehearsal without an objective in mind.** What, specifically, are you focusing on in the runthough? Transitions? Polishing choreography? Enunciation and projection? Rhythm and tempo of the scenes? Set changes? Characterization? Emotional tone? You simply cannot fix everything at once and you certainly can't assess all aspects of your show at each runthrough.

"I'm reviewing the situation..."
Lionel Bart, Oliver!

Start with obvious problems. If the dance numbers are a bit rough and the entrances and exits noisy and chaotic, conduct a rehearsal for the express purpose of fixing that. And then, *tell the cast exactly what you want them to concentrate on in this rehearsal.* Don't expect them to automatically know what you're looking for. You waste an entire rehearsal if, when you give notes, you say: "Can't you do something about the exit in the first big number? It's awful!—clumsy, unorganized—and all I can hear is shuffling feet!"

First, there are more positive ways to give constructive criticism! (See Appendix A, Dear Director...) and secondly, your cast is liable to react with the thought: "Well, if she had wanted us to do that, why didn't she tell us *before?* We would have fixed it!"

A good prompt before a rehearsal might be: "During this rehearsal, I'm going to be checking for enunciation and projection. *You* know the words. *I* know the words. But will the *audience* understand you? They don't know the story. You must tell it anew, with great clarity *every* time. I am your audience. Pretend that I am hard-of-hearing, barely understand English and forgot my glasses at home." Then, when you're giving notes from that rehearsal, if you say: "I understood every word that Tevye and Tzeitel said, but I'm still having trouble hearing Golde," the characters can digest the information and fix it for next time.

Pacing Rehearsals

The rhythm and tempo of a production can have far-reaching effects on the success of your show. Most shows come off amateurish not because they were badly acted or sung, but because the energy was just not there. The show dragged. The challenge for the director, is to pick up the tempo of a show without the actors rushing their lines. This can be accomplished by picking up cues faster, building the tempo of each scene from beginning to end, speeding up set changes, smoothing transitions and keeping concentration and energy levels high. If one actor loses focus, it tends to be contagious and a scene can easily slow until it grinds, painfully, to a halt.

This can happen while the cast is "holding" for applause after a musical number. Actors should not acknowledge appreciation in any way, but, if they continue, the audience may miss important dialogue. They should simply freeze and wait until the applause begins to wane, then resume the scene. The danger during this hold is for minds to wander. An amateur cast should be reminded that this is not a good time to rest or think about what they're having for a late snack when they get home! They need to keep up concentration and energy and think about the next moment.

PRODUCTION WEEK: TECH AND DRESS REHEARSALS

FRIDAY	SATURDAY	SUNDAY	MONDAY	TUESDAY	WEDNESDAY	THURSDAY	FRIDAY
Lighting Tech Rehearsal 6:00pm 9:00pm	Work Day Tech Crews 10:00am-4:00pm	Work Day Tech Crews 10:00am-2:00pm	Sound Crew Set Up 12:00pm-5:00pm	Dress Rehearsal with Costumes Lights Spots Sound Props and Leads in Make-up	Dress Rehearsal with Orchestra Costumes Lights Spots Sound Props Full Make-up	FINAL DRESS REHEARSAL with Orchestra Lights Spots Sound Props Costumes Make-up	OPENING NIGHT!
	Costume Parade 2:00pm-5:00pm	Work Rehearsal w/Orchestra 2:00pm-5:00pm	Sound Tech Rehearsal 5:30pm-7:00pm	Leads: 6:00pm call	Leads: 6:00pm call	Leads: 5:30pm call	Curtain: 8:00pm
	Orchestra Rehearse Alone 2:00pm-5:00pm	Set Crew Rehearsal 5:00pm-7:00pm	Complete Runthrough with Sound and Lights 7:30pm-10:00pm	Company: 7:00pm call	Supports: 6:30pm call	Supports: 6:00pm call	BREAK A LEG!
	Complete Runthrough 6:00pm-9:00pm (in costume)	Spot Rehearsals 6:00pm-8:00pm		Curtain: 8:00pm	Chorus: 7:00pm call	Chorus: 6:30pm call	
					Curtain: 8:00pm	Curtain: 8:00pm	

If the cast must move or exit after this hold, the orchestra can pick up the pace (literally) by repeating a few bars of the song or, if a mood change is necessary, a few bars of the next song. Unless you're using piano-only for accompaniment, these musical "bridges" need to be worked out by the conductor in advance and the orchestra given specific instructions.

The Speed Rehearsal

One of my favorite techniques for picking up the energy and pace of a show is the speed rehearsal. (It is also effective for exposing actors who don't know lines, lyrics, blocking, entrances, exits, etc.). A speed rehearsal is exactly that—a very fast rehearsal! All dialogue, songs, dances, changes, etc., are performed double-time. A great time to have this rehearsal is when the cast is in a rut—tired, low-energy, bored and boring. (And, believe me, by this stage in production, they will be.)

The speed rehearsal will not polish dances, improve diction or help scene transitions. And characterization will go right out the window. This rehearsal will be fast and furious, chaotic and crazy, and above all, FUN. It will bouy spirits, restore a long-lost sense of humor and release pent-up tension and stress. Be sure to warn the cast about safety. The rule is: Everyone must remain in control.

Spot Rehearsals

As you conduct runthrough rehearsals—fixing problems, adding details and polishing the show, you will find scenes or musical numbers which need additional attention. If, after repeated notes, one actor is having trouble staying in character, or the waltz for the two principals needs work, don't keep the entire cast standing around while you fix the problem. Ask the people involved to come early for rehearsal or set up another time. Budget time in the schedule for spot rehearsals on a work day when the tech people are working on the scenery or lights.

Occasionally, an entire scene or production number needs attention. In this case, you must use regular rehearsal time to fix the problem. It's a good idea to integrate the scene back into the show as soon as possible with an immediate runthrough of the show.

Technical Rehearsals

Tech rehearsals are for adding the extras—sound, lighting, orchestra, etc.—to the production. I use the term "extras" here loosely. Though I do not wish to offend the great technical directors of the world, it is true that acting, singing, dancing and costumes are the "essentials" of a musical. You could, if necessary, perform the show setless, soundless and lightless outside under a tree. (Although I am certainly not advocating that you do so!) In fact, I've been accused by my technical directors of "expecting the moon." The more lights, the better, for it is this wizardry of tech that adds much of the magic to a musical. It's the stuff that makes a show gleam and sizzle with life and spectacle.

Technical rehearsals, however, have nothing to do with spectacle. They are tedious, exhaustive and time consuming. *And,* they are necessary. If they are well organized and conducted in a professional, businesslike manner, they will be productive and relatively painless.

The most important thing to remember is this: During technical rehearsals, nothing else matters except the aspect of tech you are working on. A rehearsal to set the lights is just that, a rehearsal to set the lights. If it is an orchestra rehearsal, who cares if all the costume parts are matching, and if it's a sound rehearsal, make-up doesn't matter! You will not assess characterization, enunciation or any other part of the show.

Tempers may flare during this time. The technical people have been busily creating, planning and working on their aspect of the show behind the scenes all during the rehearsal time. No one except the director and designers have paid any attention to them. Now it's their turn.

And, the actors, who have had center stage (literally) for weeks, must now become nameless, faceless bodies. Their sole function is to do what the technical director or stage manager tells them. "Move three steps *left.* That's it. Can you find the hot spot there? Remember where it is. You won't be able to go any further *downstage* or you'll be out of the light. Got that?" Most of the cast will be patient, perhaps even fascinated. But after two hours of this, the most even-keeled can get crotchety. Your ability to focus on each task and keep the traffic moving will relieve the stress and prevent ruffled feathers.

Five Technical Aspects of the Musical

There are five areas of tech which require separate and careful attention during tech week. They are: costumes, lighting, sound, orchestra and make-up. By now, props should already be fully integrated into the show and, the sets and scenery are in use and have been continually assessed during the runthrough rehearsals. Both of these areas will need to be evaluated, but do not require a separate time slot.

The Costume Parade

The costume parade could not accurately be called a rehearsal. It is a scene-by-scene walk-through in costume of the entire show by every cast member. In attendance is the director, the costume designer and the make-up, set and lighting designers. The purpose of the costume parade is to make a detailed assessment of each costume to be worn in the show. Ideally, by this point, all cast members will have every costume piece, shoe and accessory.

The costume designer, notebook in hand, sits in the audience and watches the parade go by. What does he or she look for?

FIT: Does each costume fit properly? Consider hem-length, sleeve-length and mobility. Because of the importance of dancing in a musical, this is a major issue. The choreographer may want to make notes about this.

COMPLETENESS: Is every piece of each costume there? Pay close attention to shoes, socks, hats, scarves, ties, belts, purses, and other accessories. Make a detailed list.

COLOR: Does the color scheme of each costume work? Does it convey the intended meaning? Do the costumes work on the set? The set designer should make notes. It may be easier to repaint trim on the set than to rebuild a costume.

Do the costumes work together visually? To assess this, all characters who appear in a scene must be evaluated *together* as well as separately.

Do the costumes work under stage lighting? Although the lighting will not be finalized at this point, the lighting designer can make notes about intensity and colorization. This will save time at the lighting tech rehearsal.

DETAIL: Do the costumes transmit needed information? Are the buttons, cuffs, trim, texture and other details large enough to be seen from the back row? You don't have time to rebuild entire costumes but, you could easily modify details and change accessories.

STYLE: Are all costumes and accessories in the correct historical period or style? It can be easy to miss these details, especially, in crowd scenes if you don't look for them specifically. However, your audience will notice if townspeople in Anatevka are wearing Adidas!

CONSISTENCY: Do all costumes within a group work together? This is especially important in chorus scenes. Since we already know that the audience will focus on the one thing which is different, it will not do to have eleven ladies in the chorus line wearing black stockings and one wearing brown. These problems are easy to identify and usually simple to fix. Your attention to detail at this stage again crosses that fine line between a so-so and a wonderful production.

In a large show with a cast of many, the costume parade can be a very frustrating experience. The cast has known for weeks which pieces of their costumes they must procure and by when. And yet, they will repeatedly show up onstage without major items. "Where are your shoes?" asks the director. "I haven't gotten them yet." "Why haven't you? We open in six days!" They never have a satisfactory answer nor do they seem to be especially concerned about the problem. And threats of replacing the actor usually don't help at this point.

One solution I've used successfully is to have two costume parades—one, two weeks before opening and the other, one week before, for final check. This takes up three more hours of valuable time, but dramatically increases the chances that you'll have a show with complete costumes down to the last piece of ricrac. And, of course, there's always the chance that the miracle will occur and they'll all show up with everything the first time! I've said that if this ever happened I'd have reached the peak of my directing career and I'd hang up my yellow notebook. I'm still waiting.

The Lighting Rehearsal

Most of the major work on lighting will have been accomplished during work days as the set was being constructed. And, as rehearsals progressed, the lighting designer and technicians will have been experimenting with lighting areas and levels (intensity). In other words, the lights are hung and there is light on the set. However, it is necessary, to set aside a specific period of time to adjust the areas, refocus lights, hang special effects lighting, assess colorization and attend to other details.

In order for the lighting people to accomplish this, they need live bodies onstage to light. This can be an unpleasant experience from the point of view of the actor. It is tiresome, hot, seems to take forever and appears to be a waste of time. The director's attitude can make or break this rehearsal. If it is approached with a *"this will seem tedious, but we want the technical aspects of our show to shine as brightly as our singing, dancing, and acting. . ."* attitude, the cast is likely to respond more positively.

In addition, be sure that your lighting people are ready for this rehearsal. They need to have done as much preliminary work as possible *before* the tech rehearsal. And, conduct this rehearsal purposefully and briskly. It is not a time to stop and discuss the virtues of using magenta vs. indigo gels. Make a decision, adjust the instruments and move on to the next scene. There will be time to assess the effects later and make changes if necessary.

There are several specific aspects of lighting which should be dealt with at this rehearsal:

AREAS: Are all acting areas fully lit in each scene? To determine this, actors need to be in position. You can't tell by looking at the light cast on the bare set. If you discover a "dead spot" additional lighting instruments may have to be hung or other instruments redirected. Do this as quickly as possible. It is usually not possible to light every square inch of every scene. Aim for *most* of the actors in *most* of the scenes to be fully lit *most* of the time.

INTENSITY: How brightly do you want each scene lit? In most cases this can be decided approximately before the tech rehearsal and experimented with at runthrough rehearsals. You may, however, have to take tech rehearsal time to set levels for some scenes. Come to an agreement with your technical directors and designers, set the level, write it down, then, assess it later during dress rehearsals.

SPECIAL EFFECTS: Projections on a screen or scrim, lighting a cyclorama and other dramatic lighting effects on the set can be done at some other time. Tech rehearsal time should be spent on lighting actors. If you want an effect such as moonlight on an actor's face, special shadowing or the dramatic effects of backlighting, set these at the tech rehearsal.

COLORIZATION: What color wash do you want for each scene? As previously mentioned, gels can be in place before the tech rehearsal so that little if any time need be spent other than agreeing on its workability.

SPOT LIGHTS: I generally do not deal with follow spots at all during the rehearsal. There is time during dress rehearsals to add spots and make adjustments. However, if you plan to use them, keep in mind that their intensity will tend to wash out other stage lighting and may cast unwanted shadows on the stage. Since they are mainly used for solo scenes, set aside a time for your principals to be on the set rather than keep your whole cast idle while you make decisions.

A note about beginning actors and lighting: Do not assume that the amateur actor understands stage lighting and how to stay in the light. Unless you explain about "finding the hot spot" and ignoring the light on the floor, they may go unlit through the entire run of the show.

One last thing about the lighting rehearsal. Save a lot of frustration and yelling by requiring your actors to be silent during this rehearsal. This is not a time for visiting. The only voices that should be heard are the directors', designers' and the technicians'. This holds true for all of the technical rehearsals.

The Sound Rehearsal

Because of the significance of sound in a musical, this tech rehearsal is of major importance. Up to now, you have been relying on enunciation, projection and acting technique to get the message to the back row. Now it's time to enhance and amplify the sound in preparation for adding the orchestra.

This is not as simple as flipping a switch and doing a runthrough. The cast must learn to deal with a whole new set of problems and obstacles.

All equipment—microphones, amplifiers, speakers, receivers, other equipment and the accompanying miles of cord—should be installed *before* the sound rehearsal at a time when the cast isn't present. Unless you're lucky enough to have a built-in sound system, this can take anywhere from three to eight hours or more, so reserve a time in your schedule.

Then, when the actors arrive for the rehearsal, you can start training them to handle the equipment. Dealing with microphones is the biggest challenge. Each type of mike has its own problems and idiosyncrasies. If you are using several different types for the show, even the veteran actors will need instruction.

Lesson number one: All microphones are unidirectional—pick up sound from one point, or omnidirectional—pick up sound from all sides. Actors need to know how they work so they can position their bodies and direct sound toward the microphones. This holds true whether you use stationary mikes, suspended mikes, hand-held remotes or clip-on remotes.

The least expensive, most common mikes are stationary mikes on stands. They also can be the toughest to work with because they generally pick up sound in a cone-shaped area and, if the actors do not position themselves within that area, they will not be heard. If this is your only option, be sure the actors are aware of this.

Suspended mikes have the same problems. However, it is diminished by the fact that they are hung some distance above the stage and therefore the cone or area which can be picked up is larger. An additional problem occurs because they are aimed directly at the floor of the stage and can easily pick up unwanted foot noise. Amateur casts are typically heavy-footed anyhow, so be aware of this.

As I mentioned in Chapter 12, there are only a handful of shows where you could realistically use remote hand-held mikes. If they work in your show, the challenge for the actors will be speaking or singing directly into the mike and handling them between numbers and during exits and entrances.

The best sound amplification system (and, unfortunately, the most expensive) is a remote system which utilizes clip-on microphones. Even this high-tech equipment isn't without difficulties. In fact I think they could offer an entire college course on the proper use of clip-on remotes.

First problem: They use expensive batteries—about one for every hour of operation. Second problem: The equipment is so sensitive, that if the levels are not set properly, feedback may be created when two actors get too close to each other. There goes the love scene!

Actors must also be careful during costume changes not to turn off the mike accidently. If they do, it can be very distracting to watch them dig around under their costumes to turn it on. And, if the technician forgets to turn off a mike, the audience may be privy to costume changes, backstage comments and other embarrassing dialogue which is not included in the price of the ticket. Yes, this is one of those mistakes that wasn't in the book!

All of these problems are purely logistical and can be avoided. The more time an actor has to work with the mikes, the less likely he is to have problems with the equipment. And, the better the technicians know the show, the less likely they are to make mistakes. Use the tech rehearsal to learn to handle the equipment and overcome these obstacles *before* opening night.

The Orchestra Rehearsals

There are three stages to orchestra rehearsals: orchestra alone, orchestra with cast singing but no acting, and orchestra with cast in a full runthrough of the production. Each type of rehearsal is necessary and requires a special time-slot in your production schedule.

The conductor will hold the first rehearsal. It need not be in the theatre where the performance will take place. The band room at the local high school or any other large hall will suffice. The purpose of this rehearsal is to hammer out the notes, make cuts, set tempos and dynamic levels, and deal with any irregularities in the score. Most musicals are scored by hand and, even if they are readable (and often they're not), there are always discrepancies and problems—a forgotten measure here, a missing sharp there.

The director does not need to attend this rehearsal, however, I like to make an appearance to welcome the musicians and satisfy my curiosity. Up to this point, they have only been names and phone numbers on a legal pad. It is exciting to see them putting their instruments together, adjusting reeds, rosining bows and tuning the tympani. Usually I don't stay long. I've found that their first runthrough of the music usually doesn't measure up to my standards even if they are professional musicians. This is understandable—I wouldn't want them to judge my show based on the first rehearsal, either!

"Seventy-six trombones led the big parade..." ### Meredith Willson, The Music Man

The second rehearsal will be conducted with the cast in chairs onstage in the performance hall. No costumes, make-up, props, lighting, dancing, or acting. Only singing. The transition from piano accompaniment to full orchestra is a giant leap—the fewer distractions, the better. Besides learning to deal with a completely new sound, the cast should be made aware of several other specific problems.

EYE CONTACT: Actors, especially principals, need to keep one eye on the conductor to insure timely entrances and accurate tempos. This can be difficult because the actor is also concentrating on characterization, choreography, and other technical problems such as microphones. It is even more of a problem in crowd scenes where most of the cast will not be able to see the conductor. This can be solved by having one actor watch the conductor and the others cue off him.

SOUND DELAY: In situations where the orchestra pit is located in front of the stage, if actors start their sound precisely with the conductor's downbeat, the audience will perceive that the voice is *late*. This is even further complicated by the fact that the orchestra sound is slightly delayed in getting to the actor! To avoid this, the actors must learn to *anticipate* the downbeat—to sing ahead of the beat. This takes practice.

CUES: A musical cue is a note or short musical phrase which signals the singer when to come in and on what pitch. At every rehearsal up to now the singers have been cued by the piano. They now need to learn to recognize cues from various other instruments in the orchestra—clarinet, oboe, trumpet, bassoon, etc. They must retrain their ears.

In addition, the introductory music or bridge music for each song will sound different. Singers need to get used to the new sound.

Extra Orchestra Rehearsals

It is ideal if the orchestra can have an additional rehearsal. The conductor will have many notes on tempo, style, dynamic levels, transitions, cuts, revisions and any other peculiarities which may have surfaced during the rehearsal with the cast. Sometimes, for financial or scheduling reasons, this is not possible. In such instances, the conductor should make a detailed list with all necessary information and changes. Encourage the musicians to read and assimilate the new information.

Full Runthroughs with the Orchestra

The last stage of orchestra rehearsals is full runthroughs onstage. These rehearsals are the most important. In fact, in some cases, they may be the *only* rehearsals with the orchestra.

The first runthrough with accompaniment may be rough—there are so many variables. Rehearse with the sound system and lighting but don't worry about make-up and costumes. The main purpose is to get used to the new sound. Concentrate on the following areas:

TEMPO: Are tempos consistent with what has previously been set?

BALANCE: Can singers be heard over the accompaniment?

TRANSITIONS: Is there enough music for the chorus to get into place for production numbers? Is additional set change music necessary?

The more rehearsals you have with full accompaniment the better. However, some groups can only afford one runthrough and one final rehearsal. With a good conductor, experienced professional musicians and a show that is well-rehearsed, this will be adequate.

Rehearsals in Make-up

Rather than have separate rehearsals to practice and evalute make-up, combine this area with dress rehearsals. It is, however, a good idea with amateur casts to have a make-up *workshop* during the rehearsal period before production week. And it will be extremely beneficial to have several practice applications before final dress rehearsal.

Dress Rehearsals

By this stage in production, all pieces of the puzzle are in place. They simply need to be adjusted, tightened, polished and brightened. You are so close. Yet, this may be the most panicky time of all. The big question: **Is every detail under control?** I've never been able to answer "yes" to this question. There are simply too many variables. If you're lucky, however, there are only small details to adjust.

In a big production, you need at least three dress rehearsals. All directors and designers should attend and take notes. What to look for?

HEARABILITY AND UNDERSTANDABILITY: Can you hear and understand all actors? Does the accompaniment overshadow the voices? Is the storyline clear? Are all actors in character? Do physicalization and stage business work?

VISUAL EFFECTIVENESS: Do compositions, picturizations work? Is the choreography clean and polished? Do the set and costumes work together? Is the lighting adequate? Effective?

PACING: Is the rhythm and tempo of the scenes working? Are transitions smooth and set changes fast and effective? Are there any draggy places?

ENERGY LEVEL AND VITALITY: Does the production sparkle? Is it polished? Does it seem effortless? Is the magic working?

OVERALL PICTURE: What is the overall effect? Does everything work together? Does the concept/thematic statement come through? Is there unity of idea? Does it all "fit"?

"Things look swell, things look great..."
Stephen Sondheim, **Gypsy**

As the artistic director is answering these questions, the other directors and designers can make notes also. For example, the musical director will assess enunciation, projection, intonation, harmony, etc., while the choreographer will note details of style, energy level, head and body position, extension, etc.

At the same time, designers should assess color and details such as set and costume trim, costume mobility, make-up effectiveness, etc.

At this point you can not hope to make major changes. Everything should be "set." Rather, you will note minute details, small nuances which, if adjusted, can improve the overall performance.

Examples of changes which might be effective:

LIGHTING: Addition of spots, level or color changes.

SOUND: Level changes to compensate for accompaniment, redirection of microphones.

COSTUMES: Hem-length changes, wider or bolder trim, accessory changes, faster costume changes.

SET: Faster set changes, repainting trim or adding detail, stipling, shadowing, etc.

ORCHESTRA: Balance within orchestra, overall level of dynamics, slight tempo changes, stylistic changes.

PROPERTIES: Change of color or style (example: repaint all canes red).

VOCALS: Clearer enunciation, stronger harmony, better projection, individual improvements in song delivery, addition of "holds" for applause.

CHOREOGRAPHY: Increase energy level, change head position, more extension, stylistic improvements, clean up entrances and exits of production numbers.

ACTING: Project dialogue, pacing changes, stage business bigger, exaggerate or downplay characterization.

Staging the Curtain Call

The very last thing to do before final dress rehearsal is stage the curtain call. If you have a large cast you should plan about 45 minutes for this task. It is really a matter of directing traffic. Chorus groups take their bows first, followed by actors with smallest parts, cameo roles (small, but important), supporting leads, and finally leads.

This curtain call should be brisk and organized. (In other words, rehearse it a couple of times!) In order to keep up the pace, have actors enter from both wings, meet *downstage center*, take their bows and then get out of the way for the next group. Usually, the orchestra plays one of the hit tunes from the show which they have rehearsed for this purpose. Exact timing will depend on the audience. If they really like a particular character, he or she should acknowledge the applause graciously until it starts to subside, then on with the next group.

When all actors have accepted their accolades, they should acknowledge the conductor and the orchestra and then take a final company bow.

During final performances and in school and community groups, directors and other personnel are often acknowledged also. Be prepared for anything—it is the enthusiasm of your audience which will dictate the length and character of the curtain call.

"Tonight, tonight, won't be just any night..."
Leonard Bernstein, West Side Story

Final Dress Rehearsal

The final dress rehearsal is just like a performance, including all technical aspects, full accompaniment, lighting, etc. It is a dry run of opening night. Many groups like to invite special guests—local press, school personnel, etc. It's good to have an audience to play to. Also, assuming that you've got a great show, those who see the "sneak preview" can spread the word.

I do not subscribe to the "bad dress rehearsal—good opening performance" myth. A poor dress rehearsal usually signals lack of concentration, or not enough rehearsal. I expect a *great* dress rehearsal. Knowing my expectations, and being the overachievers that amateur casts generally are, the cast usually comes through.

"Peaking Too Soon"

There is a theory in theatre that you need to be careful of "peaking too soon"—that is, reaching your highest level of performance BEFORE opening night. There is some validity to this with amateur productions because inexperienced actors tend not to have the discipline to sustain a high level of performance indefinitely. Perhaps this is because they've worked so hard that, when they finally get there, they tend to relax in relief and exaltation.

A good director can pace final rehearsals so that the performance "arrives," skill-wise and energy-wise, on opening night. This is largely a function of attitude and enthusiasm. You can't let up until exactly the right moment. You must use your intuition to determine when this is. Every cast and every show is different.

19 On with the Show!

Opening Night and Thereafter

Finally! The show is ready. You are ready. It's time for the big payoff. The electricity and butterflies are everywhere. No one, even the veteran actor, is immune from opening night jitters. And, it's the best feeling in the world. However, you will not be able to escape the feeling that you've forgotten something. On the following pages is a checklist and a schedule for the **VERY LAST DAY!**

> *"Luck, be a lady tonight..."*
> *Frank Loesser,* **Guys and Dolls**

Extended Runs

Whether you do two performances or twenty, it will be difficult to match the electricity of opening night. However, successive performances, though they lack the frantic fire, are often better technically. The confidence of knowing you have a successful show will relax the cast and with each repetition comes a more mature, polished show.

The difficulty will be sustaining that energy level over an extended time. This is not merely a physical challenge, it is attitudinal. If you're performing only on weekends you may need to schedule a "pick-up" rehearsal during the week to keep the performance sharp.

Most school and community shows do not run for extended periods because of expense and time factors. In addition, if you live in a small city, you may not have enough paying customers to warrant a long run. It is better to do three sold-out performances than to play to half-filled houses over an extended run.

CHECKLIST: LAST DAY

SETS AND SCENERY
___last coat of paint
___trim, stipling etc.
___mask backstage
areas
___spike floor for set
___reflective tape
___clean/sweep
___cue posters
___set pieces in place

LIGHTING
___all areas set
___lamp and bulb check
___projector bulbs
___cue sheets
___spots

SOUND
___mikes operational
___mikes properly
angled
___cords taped down
___remotes working
___new/extra batteries
___cue sheets
___carpet squares under
mike stands to
muffle vibration

COSTUMES
___all costumes clean
and in good repair
___emergency supplies -
tape, needle, thread
pins, scissors, etc.
___costume area neat
and clean
___cue posters in
dressing rooms

PROPERTIES
___all props ready and
in good working

MAKE-UP
___adequate base,
powder, hairspray
___liner pencils sharp
___kleenex, paper
towels, hairpins

ORCHESTRA PIT
___chairs and music
stands in place
___stand lights/extra
bulbs
___cords and electrical
connections checked

COMMUNICATIONS SYSTEM
___system working
___headsets for all
crew heads - stage
manager, conductor
___extra batteries

BOX OFFICE
___ticket inventory
___change box
___ticket collectors
___ushers
___playbills ready

THE FINAL COUNTDOWN

8:00 a.m.   final coat of paint (latex!)
last minute details

3:00 p.m.   TECHNICAL CHECKS
sets and scenery
lighting
sound
properties
costumes
make-up
orchestra
backstage
box office

5:30 p.m.   LEADS MAKE-UP CALL
(earlier, if necessary for hair, beards or
complex make-up)

6:00 p.m.   SECOND MAKE-UP CALL
(usually supporting leads and secondary
characters)

6:15 p.m.   TECH RECHECK

6:45 p.m.   MIKE CHECK/BATTERY CHECK

7:00 p.m.   BOX OFFICE OPENS
CURTAIN CLOSES (no actors out front)
PHYSICAL WARM-UPS BEGIN
USHERS REPORT
ORCHESTRA WARM UP

7:15 p.m.   HOUSE OPENS
VOCAL WARM-UPS

7:30 p.m.   FINAL NOTES/WORDS OF WISDOM

7:45 p.m.   FINAL TECH CHECK
ACTORS QUIET TIME (check costumes etc.)

7:55 P.M.   "PLACES..."

8:00 p.m.   OVERTURE - CURTAIN OPENS!

AFTER PERFORMANCE CHECKLIST

SETS AND SCENERY
____return rented/
borrowed items
____store unit set
pieces
____dismantle unstorable
set pieces (keep re-
usable lumber)
____store or return
drops, cycloramas
scrims etc.
____inventory new set
pieces
____clean stage and
backstage areas

SOUND AND LIGHTING
____dismantle sound
system
____return rented/
borrowed equipment
____store spots and
lighting instruments
____rehang and readjust
instruments

COSTUMES
____clean and store
____add new costumes
to inventory
____return rented/
borrowed costumes

and accessories
____clean dressing areas

ORCHESTRA
____return scores to
conductor (no score,
no paycheck!)
____store or return
music stands,
lights, cords etc.
____clear pit area

SCRIPTS AND SCORES
____inventory and return
rented scripts and
scores to company

BOOK-KEEPING
____count receipts
____pay orchestra, sound
technicians, etc.
____pay outstanding
debts

HOUSE AND BOX OFFICE
____clean seating and
box office areas

Tying Up Loose Ends

Even when it's over, it's not over. After the last curtain falls on the last performance, there is yet more to be done. And, this may be the hardest work of all because the thrill is gone—you're simply tying up loose ends. It's like picking up the morning after a big party—cleaning, sorting and putting away. Even when you're tired and uninspired, it must be done.

There's a sign in a lake cabin in Ontario, Canada, which reads: "*Every good camper leaves the camp in as good or better shape than he found it.*" So it is with a theatre. Whether it's your building or a rented performance hall, you must return it to working order.

Is There Life after "Superstar"?

For professional actors and theatre people, the end of a show merely signals a rest—or perhaps, a preparation period for the next production. For school and community theatre people, the final curtain is really an *end*. Their work, home, and social lives have been on hold while they piled themselves a hundred percent into this project. At the end of such an investment—after the exhilaration (and along with the relief)—can come emptiness, sadness and depression. This can be compared to what psychologists call "separation anxiety." It is experienced by war buddies, survivors of a disaster, any group who has bonded together to overcome extreme obstacles.

So, if you find yourself moping about singing "Don't Cry for Me Argentina" or interjecting bits of dialogue from the show into everyday conversation, you're not going insane. It's natural. You *will* get over it. You'll take with you wonderful memories and the knowledge that you participated in one of the most thrilling, challenging experiences of the American Theatre—the Broadway Musical. *And*, you did it—**Way Off Broadway!**

"*So long, farewell, auf wiedersehen, good bye...*"
Oscar Hammerstein II, The Sound of Music

A Dear Director. . .

Helpful Hints on Rehearsal
Techniques and Relationships

When everything else is said and done and all creative and technical aspects of the show are under control, it is your expertise at dealing with people—*your ability to communicate and influence*—which will make the difference between an average performance and a hit. As a director, you are not an island. Your relationships with actors, design and technical staff, other directors, and anyone connected with the production are important.

On these pages I offer helpful hints and suggestions on relationships and other aspects of directing a musical which do not neatly fit into any other category.

On Giving Notes

The purpose of giving notes to actors and technical crews is to affect change in performance to improve the production in some way. In other words, you take note of what's wrong and try to fix it. You, as director, must look critically at every aspect of the production. However, being *critical* does not necessarily mean being *negative*. In fact, you'll get better results by pointing out the *good* things.

For example, if your goal is to get the character Kurt in *The Sound of Music* to keep his head up so his voice projects and he doesn't cast shadows on himself, try saying, "I'm really impressed with the way Brigitta keeps her head up every minute. Not only can I see her, I can understand every word she says. Good job!" You'll be surprised at the effect that statement has on the head position of the entire cast.

A word of caution: When you do this, give honest, sincere appreciation.

Be sure the praise is justified or the technique will backfire and the cast will assume you don't know good from bad acting.

You will, of course, have to speak directly to some problems, and you can still approach them positively. If an actor continues to mumble his lines after you've tried the group approach, try saying, "John, it is imperative that you spit out those consonants in the opening speech. The audience *must* understand you," instead of, "John, I can't understand a word you're saying. You know better than that! What's the matter with you?"

Most directors do understand the power of the positive *and* they should be especially aware of it during final rehearsals when bodies are tired and skins are thinner.

Number of Notes

The closer you get to opening night, the more notes you will have, even though it would seem to be just the opposite. In the first complete runthrough there are so many things to fix that you can not possibly recognize them all, much less record them. As rehearsals progress and the show improves on all fronts, you will be able to focus on specific, fixable problems. It is when you can pick out little details that you're getting close to performance readiness. Explain this to your cast because they won't understand why you have 45 minutes of notes three days before opening night. They will just think you're being "picky."

When to Give Notes

The end of a grueling three-hour rehearsal is *not* the best time to give notes. Yes, the rehearsal will be fresh in their minds, however, their minds and bodies won't be and the cast will not be able to absorb the information and make the changes. Instead, make time for notes *before the next rehearsal*.

Note-taking Tips

Learning to view a rehearsal and verbalize the problems in short, concise language is a skill. First tip: Don't try to take notes yourself. If you're writing, you're not looking at the stage. And, if you write in the dark without looking you will not be able to decipher what you've written. Find an assistant to sit beside you as you view the rehearsal. You watch and dictate the notes to them. It is helpful if they have good hearing, good penmanship and some knowledge of the show.

Be brief and specific. Following are examples of notes. The statement in parenthesis is what I would add as I deliver the notes to actors.

FAGIN: Look out more in "Reviewing." (I'm losing your face as you look into the chest.)

CAPTAIN VON TRAPP: Riding crop. (Where was it!?)

LIGHTING: More light on finale. (Bring it up about two levels.)

TOWNSPEOPLE: All eyes on Prof. Hill in gym. (We're losing focus because some of you are drifting.)

ACCOMPANIMENT: "Surrey" is draggy. (Let's pick up the tempo just a bit.)

GENERALS: Rocking chairs. (Either all of you rock on the beat or none of you!)

CHE AND EVA: Polish "Waltz." (You two need to sneak off somewhere for a few minutes before *Act II* and practice!)

PICK-A-LITTLE LADIES: Consonants! (Spit out those *P*'s, *T*'s, and *K*'s! You're supposed to be clucking chickens not purring pussy cats!)

JOHN: Great! (I don't know what you did last night, but your character has improved one thousand percent since yesterday!)

Humor can be a powerful tool of communication especially during the tired tense last weeks. Saying to the soldiers in *Evita*, "You guys look like a pack of old ladies out there! COME ON!" may be ultimately more effective than "That was the sloppiest routine I have ever seen. Fix it!"

Dealing with Difficult People

Theatre people—actors—have a reputation for being eccentric and highstrung. This is not without some validity for it takes tremendous ego strength to perform. Even the amateur actor—the local dentist or the Catholic church choir director have "self" involved. When they are tired and have been pushing themselves to the limit they may be just as "touchy" as the veteran actor with the bad reputation.

Dealing with these difficult people in difficult situations is a big part of a director's job. In fact, good directors function as psychologist, priest and nursemaid in addition to their responsibilities as creative genius. The better a director's people skills the more effective he or she will be.

Personality Types

If variety is the spice of life, then a musical production is indeed peppery. And, in a community theatre group with the varying ages, occupations and experiences, it can be quite a challenge to deal with all the "individuals" as you attempt to unify them into a working team.

Most difficult behavior is an actor's way of dealing with insecurities and the stress of performing. In order to get their best performance, you'll have to treat them as individuals. This requires a great deal of sensitivity and diplomacy. Here are a few of the unique "personalities" I have encountered and some hints on dealing with them.

PRIMA-DONNA PATTY is hot stuff. She, of course, has had big parts and may tend to think that her skills are above and beyond everyone else's. She's usually talented and adds a lot to the production. You need her. But, if you cater to her, the rest of the group may become resentful. A private talk may tone her attitude down a bit without antagonizing the other actors.

DEFENSIVE DAN does not take direction well. He has an excuse for everything and reacts negatively to suggestions, especially notes. If you are going to be critical of his performance, as of course you must, be sure to preface each note with something positive.

NERVOUS NELLIE is petrified. She has no self confidence and you'll need to praise her often. She will, if coaxed, come out of her shell eventually and be a great asset to the show.

PAT, THE PLEASER will drive you crazy. He is constantly at your elbow offering service of some sort. He wants to be noticed and truly means to be helpful. Put him to work. Give him odd jobs and responsibilities. There certainly are plenty of those.

ASPIRING AL, the self-appointed director, thinks he knows as much about directing as you do and is lavish with suggestions and advice. If you don't capitalize on his energy and expertise, he will begin to irritate you or worse—undermine your authority. Put him in charge of something—a scene, a dance, or a group of townspeople working on character.

DIFFICULT DEBBIE makes mountains out of molehills and a production out of everything. Her reaction to even the slightest problem will make you and the other actors roll eyes in disbelief. One technique is to ignore her completely. This may simply exaggerate the problem for she really craves attention. Try to be supportive and keep her busy so she'll not have time to overreact.

MAC, THE MUGGER loves to overact. If left alone his antics will be distracting and almost painful for the audience to watch. One trick I've used: Put him to work with another actor on their lines together with instructions to "underact" or play it straight. Tell him it is to help the *other* actor. Then, when the scenes start to improve, you can say, "I don't know what you're doing different, but I like it. Leave it in!" Yes, this is manipulative, but it will work and is for the good of the production.

FLAMBOYANT FLOSSIE is "bigger than Dallas." She sweeps onstage and occupies twice the space (literally and figuratively) of anyone else. If you don't tone her down, she will draw focus from other aspects of the show. Try the same trick you used on "Mac, the Mugger." The object: to get her to reign herself in onstage so she won't upstage the production.

FORGETFUL FRANCIS is scatter-brained. Never prepared, she is continually without script, pencil, costume parts and props. Ideally, you'd like to cure her but this may be too much to hope for in the course of one production. Get her a "keeper"—an organized, helpful cast member who needs a project.

RETIRING RITA is a mere shadow. Were it not for her name in the program, you might not notice her onstage at all and with so much on your mind, you might forget to *direct* her. Don't leave her out. Like "Nervous Nellie," she just needs a little coaxing and positive reinforcement.

JACK, THE JOKER is hard to direct. His way of dealing with stress is to laugh and make fun. If he happens to be one of your leads, you're in trouble because the other cast members tend to take their cue from his attitude. In a production of *Jesus Christ Superstar*, our Jesus was such a character. At a time when the entire cast needed to focus on him, he was laughing it up, most inappropriately. When subtle hints failed to reach him, I took him aside for a private talk. In this case, honesty was the best policy. "I *need* you to change your attitude and take this more seriously. Everyone else is looking to you for inspiration. You are letting them *and yourself* down."

TINA, THE TALKER never shuts up. She doesn't mean to chatter; it's her way of dealing with stress. But, she will disrupt entire rehearsals and waste valuable time if you don't curb this behavior early. She may not even realize she's talking. Speak to her privately and get another cast member or two to gently remind her.

NAT, THE NOODLE is simply limp. His total lack of energy onstage is deadly to a show, especially if he's in a scene with "Flamboyant Flossie" or "Mac, the Mugger." I've found that low-energy actors simply do not realize how they come across. Work with them on body tension during warm-ups and dance rehearsals. If this doesn't help, try the video camera.

LANCE, COME-LATELY is never on time. Whether it's because he likes to make an entrance or is just forgetful, he can lose you rehearsal time. Threats of replacing him seldom work. Give him a special job to do *before* rehearsals—a technical job such as checking props, or a clerical job like taking attendance or rewriting your notes. This added responsibility may force him to take things more seriously.

MOUSIE MARION is almost invisible. Every movement and vocal sound is minuscule. Team her up with "Flossie" for tutoring. Or, put her to work on line readings with someone who is projection personified to force her to be bigger. And, give her plenty of encouragement. She needs it.

SCREAMIN' SANDRA loses her temper at the drop of a hat and her carrying on disrupts rehearsals and can make your life miserable. Her terrible disposition is probably rooted in insecurity so try the praise approach. You may have to resort to a private talk. "I'm very impressed with your talent and and stage presence. You add a lot to the show. However, you must get better control of your emotions. I'm sure you can do it, you seem to have no trouble staying in character." If this doesn't work, her outbursts may eventually get out of hand to the point that she quits in frustration or you fire her. And, you will if you must. The success of your show may depend on it.

NEGATIVE NORRIS has nothing good to say about anything or anyone. This attitude can be deadly to the show. Try using humor. "Gosh, that was a fabulous scene. Norris, even *you* should appreciate that!" Turning his negativism around in this way may help him to view things in a better light. (Forces him to wear rose-colored glasses.) Do this gently. It may backfire if you don't.

PAUL, THE PERFECTIONIST is very hard on himself and is easily frustrated. Help him by giving him tasks which are within his capabilities, at which he can succeed and then give him positive feedback. Also, if you team him with someone who needs help, he will have to focus outward rather than on his own performance.

STAN, THE STUMBLER has two (or six) left feet. Even a simple cross will be awkward. Be aware of this limitations especially where choreography is concerned. Give him tasks at which he will be successful and extra attention during physical warm-ups and dance rehearsals. He may be the perfect "project" for Paul.

BILLIE, THE BRAGGER has been everywhere, done everything and will bore everyone to distraction with his accounts of these achievements. Usually a cover-up for insecurities, he needs a project and plenty of praise. Let him tutor "Nat, the Noodle." Keep him so busy with important responsibilities that he has no time to show off.

STRUTTIN' SUZIE never misses an opportunity to impress everyone (especially you) by practicing the most difficult dance moves or delivering brilliant soliloquies, usually at most inopportune times. You can try to ignore her or put her to work. She's probably talented and her expertise can aid other, less experienced actors.

PSYCHOMATIC PSARAH in her own words "can't do anything." She always has a bad back, a sore knee or some other ailment which keeps her from succeeding. She needs constant reinforcement. Give it to her. It is the key to her success. She will also benefit by being kept busy, perhaps by helping another actor.

LENNY, THE LOVER is the Don Juan of your production and always manages to go through three or four girlfriends in the course of the show. This in itself is not harmful; it can, however, cause disharmony amongst the female population of your cast and, if his attention is focused on the ladies, he's not likely to give his best performance in the show. You need to distract him with "bigger" things—more responsibility—for if he perceives that a task you've given him is "for the good of the show" he knows it will enhance his reputation. Yes, this is manipulative, but for a good cause. You may have to resort to a straight talk with him. His type is more likely to respond to ultimatums.

There are endless variations in personality. If you spend enough time in the musical theatre business, you will encounter them all and your people skills will be tested to the limit.

Dealing with Conflicts

I have never been involved in a production where a personality conflict didn't arise, sooner or later. You may need to wear the black and white stripes of a referee. Knowing what to expect may help you stave off problems.

Principal vs. Chorus

Every production has some friction between the leading characters and minor characters. This is not necessarily because the leading characters are "Prima-Donna Patties." It is simply that at heart, everyone wants to play the lead and there often is hidden resentment by those who didn't get the part they wanted.

You can help to avoid conflict by ensuring the *chorus* of their worth at every opportunity. In order for this to be effective, *you* must believe it. Just as a chain is only as strong as its weakest link, the *chorus* sets the tone for the whole production. Their attitude and performance level are vitally important to the success of the show.

Male vs. Female

This conflict generally has its root in relationships between members of the opposite sex in your cast who may or may not be getting along. It is difficult to expend so much time and energy together and not "get involved." The only thing you can do to prevent these conflicts from affecting the performance is to insist that the cast keep the show higher on their priority list than their relationships. This may take a few reminders or a private talk or two but it can be done.

Sometimes you encounter jealousies between male and female leads. This definitely warrants a private conference, for their attitude will affect everyone. "If you have enough discipline and skill to handle a major role, surely you can get a handle on your personal feelings."

Newcomer vs. Veteran

Every show has at least one actor who has been in thirteen shows and thinks he knows more than everyone else. Even if this is true, that attitude can irritate the novices who already have misgivings about performing. This can seriously undermine their performance. Encourage a team attitude. Pair the newcomers with the veterans in learning situations. You can prevent this conflict from adversely affecting the show with *your attitude*.

Skilled vs. Unskilled

This is different than newcomer versus veteran. In community theatre the level of skill will vary greatly. And, it can be frustrating for very talented actors to work with novices. It isn't that they are egotists. They simply want the performance to be as good as possible and they may have fears that these unskilled actors will bring down the whole production. In a way their fears are well founded. Poor performance by actors *can* affect the entire show negatively. However, the director who can accurately assess the abilities of the cast and dole out parts to match skill can prevent this problem.

Also, a director's ability to encourage the novices and keep the pros occupied with their own performance can help — it's the old educational trick of stimulating the overachievers in the class without losing the slow students.

Young vs. Old

Until I experienced it firsthand, I never would have thought this could be a problem. Consider the aging actress who still considers herself to be "ingenue material." Then, give the ingenue part to a younger, talented, beautiful actress with *less* experience. It seems petty and unrealistic. However, when you deal with self-concept and ego, anything is possible.

To prevent the conflict, give the older actress a good part if possible. Couple this with positive reinforcement. Be sure it is *deserved* praise. And, be aware of the sensitivity of the situation, especially when you are giving notes and verbal direction during rehearsal.

The opposite can sometimes occur. A young, less-experienced actor may be resentful that all the good parts are going to the older actors. Again, be diplomatic and sensitive to the problem.

Replacing Someone

No director is ever prepared for the unpleasant task of firing someone. However, you must remember that you *can* and *must* do it if it becomes necessary. How do you know if it is *necessary?* It is necessary if it is for the good of the show — if the show and all the energy and hours put into it would suffer seriously if you didn't.

An example from my own experience: We were using a combo accompaniment for a summer school production. This included keyboards, guitar, bass and drums. I had hired a bass player on the recommendation of another musician. He may have been a good player at one time, but something had happened since my friend had heard him last. His musician's "ear," so necessary to a bass player, was gone. He played *terribly* out of tune.

Had he been one of twenty musicians in a full orchestra, we might have been able to tolerate the problem. However, the bass player is the tonal foundation for a combo. If he plays out of tune, no one can find the tonal center, singers included. I had to replace him. How did I do this? I pulled him aside after the first rehearsal and said, "I'm very sorry, but due to some serious intonation problems, I can not use you for the show." I was petrified but I had no choice. The situation was such that the entire show would have been greatly compromised if I'd allowed him to play.

Firing an actor is a different problem altogether. First of all, how can you fire someone who's not *hired*?! This isn't professional theatre. Your actors are volunteers and in the case of some of my productions, they *paid* to be in the show. The answer is: You can't. However, you can do one of several things: You can prevent the situation by being a good instructional leader and a diplomat, you can act as mediator and remedy the situation as it arises, or, as a last resort, you can be strict enough, adamant enough that the actor with the problem quits of his own accord. This last choice is certainly not the best, but, you must put the needs of the entire production ahead of the needs of the one actor.

When Someone Quits

There are a variety of reasons why an actor or crew member quits a show. They may feel overwhelmed by the enormity of the task and not feel competent enough to handle the situation. There may be a personality conflict with the director or another cast member. There may be a lack of trust of the director or a lack of commitment. So many first-timers are not prepared to invest the time and energy a musical requires. They assume that since they are "just a chorus member," they don't have to work as hard. And, when they find out otherwise, they panic.

Also, there may be pressure from outside sources — job, home, school — which have nothing at all to do with the show, but, which prevent them from participating.

You, as director, can prevent some of these situations. If you are dealing with the cast on an appropriate level — where they can feel successful — they are less likely to be overwhelmed with feelings of incompetency. Your enthusiasm and positive attitude can also prevent an actor from leaving the show.

Sometimes, however, there is nothing you can do. When you assess that a cast or crew member "really means it" and is determined to quit the show, let them go gracefully. You hate to lost them, but, you are much better off replacing them (even with your second choice) than dealing with the situation for the remainder of the show.

Some General Suggestions

ALWAYS BE PREPARED. Do your director's homework — planning, analysis, blocking. Continually assess progress and make adjustments. It will not be unusual to spend two or three hours each day in *addition* to rehearsal hours.

BE POSITIVE. Your attitude — minute-to-minute, day-to-day — is contagious. If you are worried about some aspect of the production, try not to show it. Remember to mention the *good* things.

MODEL THE BEHAVIOR YOU EXPECT FROM THE COMPANY. Be on

time, be at *every* rehearsal, keep your energy level up, have a good attitude. Show strong commitment. They won't if you don't.

BE BUSINESSLIKE AND BRISK.   This does not mean stern or unfriendly. However, in order to be effective, you must keep a certain distance between you and the cast (even if they are friends). A brisk pace will keep things moving. Remember: **Time is everything**.

BE DIPLOMATIC, YET ASSERTIVE.   Calling a spade a spade is not always the most effective way to deal with people. When you criticize, preface the statement with something positive. Use the word *"and"* instead of *"but"*: *"I like what you did with that cross, and,* would you make it faster still?"

In some situations, you may have to pull rank to get what you want: **". . . because I am the director!"**

SAY "YES" TO SUGGESTIONS FROM THE CAST.   No matter their experience, they are involved at the deepest level with the production and therefore closer to problems which might arise. Take their suggestions into consideration.

BE ENTHUSIASTIC.   Yes, the director has to be a cheerleader at times. You won't lose dignity by hopping up and down gleefully when you see something wonderful.

HAVE HIGH EXPECTATIONS.   Just because this is an *amateur* production doesn't mean it has to be a *mediocre* production. Keep your expectations high, yet realistic. If *you* can't see it, if *you* don't believe in it, nobody else will.

I've used *creative visualization* techniques for years, even before I knew there was such a thing. It is a matter of being able to *see* what you want and then doing everything possible to reach that goal.

SAVE YOURSELF FROM EXHAUSTION.   *You can't do everything yourself.* Learn to delegate. If you have assembled a competent production team, don't forget to use them. And, put your cast to work. A school or community production is a team effort and they'll be willing to paint, lick stamps, run errands—whatever it takes to ensure a successful show.

SUBORDINATE PERSONAL FEELINGS TO THE GOOD OF THE SHOW.   You may run into a situation that you feel very strongly about. Be sure to examine your feelings carefully. Your primary goal is a good show. Every action should serve that purpose.

CONTINUE PERSONAL PROFESSIONAL GROWTH.   In order to keep your mind sharp and your ideas fresh, you *must* continue to learn about your craft. Never make the mistake of thinking you know all there is to know! Continually augment your "idea bank" by seeing every show, reading every script and theatre text. Remain open to new ideas.

Stimulating Creativity

As a director, you are an artist. Your goal in producing a musical should be to bring a fresh outlook to an existing work of art. Simply recreating someone else's creative vision will not satisfy you or your audience. Following are some ideas which may help you stimulate the creative process.

EXPLORE IDEAS ON PAPER: Fill whole legal pads full of ideas. Don't stop until you have every line full. You'll be able to discard obviously bad ideas. As you examine others you can cull them or expand upon them. Don't discard any scrap of paper until you can be sure you've exhausted all the possibilities.

DRAW PICTURES: Sketch. Doodle. Scribble on anything, anytime. Restaurant placemats, playbills, cocktail napkins, grocery receipts, etc.— wherever and whenever the mood strikes you.

WAKE UP THINKING: Write down everything you think of first thing in the morning—*before* you get out of bed. Early morning hours can be very fertile creatively. If you wake up with an idea in the middle of the night, write it down. You'll forget it if you wait until morning.

BE OPEN TO NEW IDEAS: Be open to the most outrageous suggestions from all sources. At first these ideas may seem worthless (and many of them will be), but you never know when a stroke of genius may be born from the mundane or the insane.

MAKE LISTS: Make lists of *everything*. They will keep you organized and on schedule. And, it's just possible that a single word on that sheet of paper could make the difference between a mediocre show and a great show.

B Obtaining Performance Rights

Musicals are written by playwrights, composers and lyricists, staged and performed by professionals and the material is copyrighted. Any party wishing to perform a musical must obtain permission from the company which holds the performance rights to that show. This usually involves paying royalties and rental fees as well as signing a performance contract.

The following companies hold the performance rights to most famous musicals:

Tams-Witmark Music Library, Inc.
560 Lexington Ave.
New York, NY 10022
(212) 688-2525

Music Theatre International
MTI Enterprises, Inc.
545 Eighth Ave.
New York, NY 10018
(212) 868-6668

Rodgers & Hammerstein Theatre Library
598 Madison Ave.
New York, NY 10022
(212) 541-6600

There are a handful of other companies which hold performance rights to musicals, but these are the main three and carry most Broadway-produced, hit musical shows.

Getting the Rights

This is the basic process to follow to get permission to perform a musical:

CONTACT THE COMPANY: Write or call the company and ask for a catalogue or list of shows to which they hold the rights. Find out if they will provide perusal copies of the script and score. (In my experience, Tams-Witmark does, MTI does not.)

CHOOSE THE SHOW: Read through the scripts and scores to determine if the show fits the needs of your group. (See Chapter 1.)

FILL OUT THE FORM: The company will send you a form. When you have made your final decision, they will want to know the following information:

> choice of play
> name and nature of your group
> dates and number of performances
> number of seats in theatre
> ticket prices
> type of orchestration desired

From this information they will determine the royalty and rental fees for that show.

SIGN A CONTRACT: You will receive a contract which will state the fees (there may be a deposit required) and list the terms of the agreement. Costs vary. You will usually be required to send a check to the company with the signed contract *before* they will send any materials. **Note: Read the contract!**

RECEIVE THE MATERIALS: You should receive the scripts, scores, and orchestra parts about six weeks prior to opening night unless other special arrangements are made with the company. There will be a charge for additional weeks.

RETURN THE MATERIALS: Cost for any lost or damaged music or librettos will be deducted from your deposit. Materials need to be sent back to the company within a week of your last performance. They should be free of marks.

Most companies are fairly easy to deal with and, though time consuming, the process is usually painless. The only major problems I have encountered have been with shipping companies who have lost the scores and librettos. Just hope that you won't have to deal with that situation.

C Sample Audition Packet

The following pages contain samples of forms and information sheets which could be included in an information packet for each prospective cast member. It contains data sheets for vital statistics about prospective cast members, an auditor sheet for scoring, general information, audition and character information and a character analysis sheet. In addition, I like to provide a schedule so candidates can determine if their work and home schedules can mesh with the production schedule.

DATA SHEET: COMMUNITY ED. PRODUCT. "EVITA"

NAME (as you want it in the program): _____

TELEPHONE NUMBER: Home _____   Work _____

AGE: Under 12   12-17   18-30   31-50   Over 50

HEIGHT: _____   WEIGHT: 101-125   125-150   150-175   175-200   200+

MAILING ADDRESS: _____/_____/_____
                          P.O. or Street,   City,   Zip

PREVIOUS STAGE EXPERIENCE: (circle all that apply)

Singing: none   gradeschool   jr. high   high school   college

community choir   church   other_____

Dancing: none   ballet   jazz   tap   other_____

Number of years studied?_____

Acting: none   gradeschool   jr. high   high school   college

community theatre   professional   other_____

HAVE YOU EVER BEEN IN A MUSICAL PRODUCTION BEFORE?
(If yes, please list productions and parts you've played.)

TECHNICAL EXPERIENCE: (circle any you'd be willing to help with)

costumes   props   make-up   set-building   scene-painting

sound   lighting   publicity   fund-raising

WORK SCHEDULE: none   days   nights   other_____

List any known conflicts with the schedule:

PLEASE CONSIDER ME FOR: Leading role   Supporting Lead

Chorus   Dance Troupe   Backstage only   Everything

"Evita" — General Information

FEES: This program is part of the school district's community education program. Registration fee is $20 per person, $10 for students, and $10 for any second (or third) family member. The fees go toward production costs (royalties, music rental printing, sets, costumes, props, orchestra, etc.) and instructors' fees.

PERFORMANCES: Performances are scheduled for April 22–23 in the high school auditorium. Curtain time is 8:00 p.m. Tickets will be $5 each. Advance tickets should be available on April 1.

SCHEDULE CHANGES: We will try to adhere to the schedule as closely as possible. However, it may become necessary to add a rehearsal or change a time. When this is the case we will try to notify you as much in advance as possible. This is a difficult show and we want to be well-rehearsed!

REHEARSALS: It is *extremely important* that you attend all rehearsals. If unforeseen illness or personal emergencies arise please call and leave a message as much in advance as possible. If you already know of conflicts (especially work schedules) please indicate on the registration form. *This may affect casting*!

TECHNICAL HELP: If you or someone you know has a special talent in any of the technical areas, especially costuming, please indicate. We need help with *everything*.

Audition Information — "Evita"

WHO MUST AUDITION?:   Any person who wishes to have a leading or supporting role or be a member of the dance troupe. These roles include: Eva, Che, Peron, Magaldi, Mistress, Colonels, Aristocrats, Eva's mother, brother, and four sisters, and dance troupe.

WHAT DO I DO?:   For singing roles: Sing any song of your choice, with or without accompaniment. If you need piano accompaniment, please bring the sheet music if you have it or make arrangements with the accompanist in advance. You may sing to a cassette tape. (No voices allowed on the tape.) During call-back auditions, you will be asked to sing specific numbers from the show. Music will be furnished in advance and accompaniment will be provided at the audition.

DANCE AUDITION: Leads, supports and dance troupe must audition. You will be asked to go through a movement sequence in a group. (Please wear appropriate footwear and clothes.)

CHORUS: Members of the chorus do *not* have to sing alone, but we would like to hear you. (So, grab a buddy and go for it!)

AUDITION SCHEDULE: Initial Auditions — Tuesday, 7:30 p.m. at the high school auditorium. Call-back Auditions — Wednesday, 6:30 p.m. at the same location. **NOTE: If you absolutely can *not* be at these auditions, please let us know so we can try to hear you.** This applies to chorus, only. All leads and supporting roles must be heard at the regular audition time.

Character Information Sheet—"Evita"

EVA: (G below middle C thru high A!) Born Eva Duarte, illegitimate, poor. The show chronicles her life from age 15 through her death at age 33 of cancer. Role requires extensive singing (huge range) and dancing. Must be able to portray wide age range.

CHE GUEVARA: (tenor) The legendary revolutionary, he acts as a narrator. Would have been in his late teens, early twenties. Very demanding role vocally and theatrically.

JUAN PERON: (high baritone) When Peron and Eva met, he was one of the powerful military officers in the new Argentine government. In the course of the show he becomes President of Argentina. Age: late forties, early fifties.

AUGUSTIN MAGALDI: (tenor) A Latin tango singer, late thirties, who is the first man to become of use to Eva. Her first lover, he takes her to the big city of Buenos Aires.

MISTRESS: (mezzo soprano) Sixteen years old, she was Peron's mistress at the time of his meeting with Eva. Eva deposes her.

OFFICERS: (bass/baritone) Right-wing group of military colonels high up in the Argentine government. There are four not counting Peron.

*ARMY: (baritone/tenor) Argentine army, opposed to Eva, a "mere woman," gaining such power in their government. They think she has emasculated their Colonel Peron. (8–10 soldiers) This group needs to dance!

*ARISTOCRATS: (soprano, alto, tenor, baritone, bass) Wealthy, highborn Argentines vehemently opposed to Eva's new position of power because of her lowly, illegitimate birth. (6–10) Vocally demanding—lots of harmony.

*EVA'S FAMILY: Mother, brother, and four sisters (Eva is the youngest). They help convince Magaldi to take Eva to the city. Some harmony.

*SECRET POLICE: "Heavies/thugs" from the Peronist regime—"enforcers" of policy. (2)

*EVA'S EX-LOVERS: Series of boyfriends that Eva uses in her rise from lowly nobody to successful model, radio and film star, and finally, first lady of Argentina at age 27. (6–10) Various voice ranges, some harmony.

*EVA'S DRESSERS: Eva gets the full makeover before embarking on her "rainbow" tour of Europe. This same group are also her embalmers at death. (6–8)

*PEOPLE AND WORKERS OF ARGENTINA: "Descamisados" (the shirtless ones)—Eva's champions, the working people, union members, etc. (Group of unlimited size.)

CHILDREN'S CHOIR: Group of children (age 5–13) who adore Eva, they sing "Santa Evita." (I will use up to 40 children!)

---

*It is possible, in fact *necessary*, for some cast members to be in more than one group.

Auditor #: 1 2 3 4 5

A U D I T I O N   S H E E T

NAME: _____(as you wish it to appear in the program)

HEIGHT: _____ WEIGHT: 100-125 125-150 150-175 200+

HAIR: Brown Black Blonde Red Grey Other_____

EYES: Brown Blue Green Grey Hazel Other_____

PART DESIRED: _____

SINGING	DANCING

VOICE RANGE: _____   BODY TYPE: A   B

RHYTHM: 1 2 3 4 5   RHYTHM: 1 2 3 4 5

PITCH: 1 2 3 4 5   GRACE: 1 2 3 4 5

QUALITY: 1 2 3 4 5   STYLE: 1 2 3 4 5

DICTION: 1 2 3 4 5   CARRAIGE: 1 2 3 4 5

PROJECTION: 1 2 3 4 5   LEARN ABIL: 1 2 3 4 5

ABILITY: 1 2 3 4 5   ABILITY: 1 2 3 4 5

STAR QUAL. 1 2 3 4 5   PERSONALITY: 1 2 3 4 5

COMMENTS:

LEAD _____
SUPPORT _____
CHORUS _____
DANCER _____

Character Analysis

Be sure to write this *after* you have read the play. Use as much as you can of what you learn in the play (primary sources). Use your imagination and what is implied in the text to supply missing details (secondary sources).

Physical Appearance

Age
Facial appearance (example: handsome, swarthy, plain, cute, etc.)
Height and weight
Vitality (healthy, energetic, listless, strong, etc.)

Environment (now and in the past)

What kind of family life (now and in the past)?
What was your childhood like?
Are you married? Any children? Parents?
Economic condition? Rich? Poor?
Occupation?
Are you a leader? A follower?
Sociability? Popular? A loner? Make friends easily?

Emotional and Psychological Make-up

Strong or domineering personality? Weak or submissive?
Emotional control? Even temper? Quick temper?
Selfish? Unselfish? How do you feel about other characters?

Philosophical and Religious Beliefs

How do you regard life? What are your political beliefs? Religious beliefs?
Optimistic? Pessimistic? Conservative? Liberal?

Intellect and Education

How much education have you had? Are you scientific?
Mechanical? Artistic? Creative? Are you handy at a trade?

Character Traits You Will Emphasize

Gestures, Speech, Posture, etc.

Possible Costume and Make-up

Bibliography

There are hundreds of theatre texts on producing, directing, acting, technical aspects, etc. The following list is by no means complete. However, these are books which I have found helpful in producing shows with school and community groups.

Bay, Howard. *Scene Design*. New York: Drama Book Specialists (Publishers), 1978.

Burris-Meyer, Harold, and Edward C. Cole. *Scenery for the Theatre*, 2nd revised edition. Boston: Little, Brown and Co., 1972.

Cohen, Robert, and John Harrop. *Creative Play Direction*. Englewood Cliffs, NJ: Prentice-Hall, 1974.

Corson, Richard. *Stage Make-up*, 6th edition. New York: Drama Books, 1982.

Craig, David. *On Singing Onstage*. New York: Schirmer Books, 1978.

Dean, Alexander, and Lawrence Carra. *Fundamentals of Play Directing*, 4th edition. New York: Holt, Rinehart and Winston, 1980.

Green, Stanley. *Broadway Musicals, Show by Show*. Milwaukee, WS: H. Leonard Books, 1985.

Grote, David. *Script Analysis*. Belmont, CA: Wadsworth, 1984.

————. *Staging the Musical: Organizing, Planning, and Rehearsing the Amateur Production*. Englewood Cliffs, NJ: Prentice Hall, 1986.

————. *Theatre: Preparation and Performance*. Glenview, IL: Scott, Foresman, 1989.

Hodge, Francis. *Play Directing: Analysis, Communication, and Style*. Englewood Cliffs, NJ: Prentice-Hall, 1971.

Hoggett, Chris. *Stage Crafts*. New York: St. Martin's Press, 1975.

Humphrey, Doris. *The Art of Making Dances*. New York: Grove Press, 1978.

Kenton, Warren. *Stage Properties and How to Make Them*, revised edition. New York: Drama Book Specialists (Publishers), 1978.

Kosarin, Oscar. *The Singing Actor: How to Be a Success in Musical Theater and Nightclubs.* Englewood Cliffs, NJ: Prentice-Hall, 1983.

Laughlin, Haller, and Randy Wheeler. *Producing the Musical: A Guide for School, College, and Community Theatres.* Westport, CT: Greenwood Press, 1984.

Lynch, Richard Chigley. *Musicals!: A Directory of Musical Properties Available for Production.* Chicago, IL: American Library Association, 1984.

Motter, Charlotte Kay. *Theatre in High School: Planning, Teaching, Directing.* Englewood Cliffs, NJ: Prentice-Hall, 1970.

Palmer, Richard H. *The Lighting Art: The Aesthetics of Stage Lighting Design.* Englewood Cliffs, NJ: Prentice-Hall, 1985.

Parker, Oren, and Harvey K. Smith. *Scene Design and Stage Lighting,* 4th edition. New York: Holt, Rinehart and Winston, 1979.

Sellman, Hunton D., and Merill J. Lessley. *Essentials of Stage Lighting,* 2nd edition. Englewood Cliffs, NJ: Prentice-Hall, 1982.

Spolin, Viola. *Improvisation for the Theater: A Handbook of Teaching and Directing Techniques.* Evanston, IL: Northwestern University Press, 1974.

Welker, David. *Stagecraft: A Handbook for Organization, Construction, and Management.* Boston: Allyn and Bacon, 1977.

Young, John Wray. *Play Direction for the High School Theatre.* Port Washington, NY: Kennikat Press, 1973.

Glossary

a cappella: Without accompaniment.

ad lib: Improvised lines. Generally used to fill in a gap, or at the end of exit speeches to carry the actor completely off stage without interruption. Also, often indicated for mob scenes. These ad lib speeches, however, should be set and kept as a fixed part of the actor's lines. All too often "ad lib" is the unintentional result of an erratic memory.

apron: The part of the stage that projects beyond the curtain line. Valuable to monologues, variety acts and musicals. Used often for intimate staging.

arena theatre: Theatre presented on a stage that is completely surrounded by the audience which affords the audience with a more intimate theatre experience.

auditor: Person who judges an audition. In a musical, this is usually the artistic director, musical director, choreographer and may include the producer and other designers.

aside: A speech made for the benefit of the audience, and presumably unheard and unnoticed by the other actors.

back drop: The curtain at the rear of a stage set. Often painted as scenery and used in musicals and melodramas.

backing: A flat piece of scenery used to mask the openings of doors and windows on the set.

backstage: That part of the stage which is invisible to the audience.

batten: A pipeline suspended from the grid, which can be raised or lowered at will. Used for suspending scenery and lighting instruments.

bit: A small part in a play. Not necessarily unimportant, and if badly done, may ruin the total effect of the production.

blackout: To turn off all the stage lights simultaneously.

blocking: The planned moves used by an actor as he performs. Blocking is usually given explicitly by the director.

border: Both the strip of scenery that masks overhead lights (sometimes called the "teaser") and the strip of lights itself.

box set: A set designed with three walls, much like a room where the audience is the "fourth wall." Usually constructed of flats.

brace: A floor support for scenery, usually metal or wood.

build-up: 1. To play a scene progressively toward a climax or 2. Centering attention upon an approaching event: "Make way for the King!"

business: Action on stage that adds to or explains the character or speeches. It must in all cases be set and not varied.

call: 1. The warning to stand by for an entrance or 2. A "curtain call," raising the curtain at the end of an act for the actors to appear in response to applause. It is preferable to permit none until the end of the play.

call-back: The second section of the audition process where the auditors select the group of actors they wish to hear again before making final casting decisions.

cast: The actors in the play.

character: The person or persons portrayed by the actor.

character analysis: The actor's study of the character he is portraying including physical and emotional characteristics, and political, social and economical background. This information is not always found in the script and may have to be inferred from the dialogue.

character part: A role in which one characteristic of the personality is overemphasized. Typical character part: drunk, old man, etc.

characterization: The actor's process of manifesting the physical and psychological traits of the character.

choreography: The staged dance and movement of musical numbers in a musical production. Generally invented by the choreographer.

chorus: In a musical, the group of actors, singers and dancers which support the leads and supporting leads. Often described as "the people of River City" or "the workers of Argentina."

clear: To free the stage of unauthorized objects or people prior to opening the curtain.

climactic composition: In blocking a scene, a configuration where two actors are standing close together (within six feet of each other) which generally sig-

nifies extreme love or hate. Directors usually save climactic compositions for the climactic moments of the show.

company: The entire cast of a musical is sometimes referred to as "the company."

cross: Movement across stage by the actor. It should be motivated and made definitely and purposefully. Usually blocked by the director.

cue: The words at the end of a speech which call for business or lines from another actor or, in a musical, notes which signal actor to begin singing.

cue sheet: Chart containing all technical cues—sound cues, lighting cues, special effects, etc., for the show. Usually contained in the stage manager's prompt book and duplicated for the crew heads.

curtain: The customary ending to a scene or act (in proscenium theatre).

cut: An elimination of part or all of a speech, piece of business or music.

cyclorama ("CYC"): A curved curtain, usually light blue, that backs the entire set, and, properly lit, gives the effect of depth.

dance troupe: The group in the chorus of a musical which does the majority of the dancing is sometimes referred to as the "dance troupe."

deadpan: An expressionless face generally assumed for comedic purposes.

dialogue: The words spoken by the actors to help develop the plot.

dimmer: A device for controlling the brightness of any light or group of lights.

downstage: Toward the audience.

drama: A literary form written to be viewed by an audience.

dressing stage: Shifting position to avoid blocking another actor from the view of an audience, or to help balance the stage picture.

drop: Short for backdrop, a large flat painted piece of scenery.

drop set: A set consisting mainly of painted drop scenery. Very popular for musicals since small scenes can take place in front of a shallow drop while bigger scenes are being set behind.

effects: (special effects): Machines for making offstage noises and visual effects (thunder, rain, wind, fog, etc.).

entr'acte: Music played by the orchestra between the acts of a musical.

EQUITY: The Equity Actors Guild is an organization of paid professional actors based in New York City.

fake: To convey the appearance of doing something, without actually doing it. Eating, drinking, fighting, etc.

fill: To improvise lines or business to cover up an unforeseen gap in performance.

fishing: Guessing at lines that an actor has not fully learned.

flats: Mounted pieces of scenery usually held in place by stage braces and lashed together.

flies: The space over the stage above the proscenium and under the gridiron upon which unused scenery is hoisted out of sight.

floods: Large high-voltage lamps used to light the stage from the wings or overhead. Can be standing or hanging.

floor cloth: A covering for the flooring of the stage.

footlights: The row of small lights set into the apron of the stage (usually amber, blue, and dark pink).

front: That part of the theater which faces the stage. "Out front" is a place actors in make-up or costume should *never* go.

gelatin (Gel): A colored piece of glass or plastic set in frames to fit lighting instruments in order to produce a special lighting effect.

gridiron (grid): The steel network above the stage from which the borders, curtains, backdrops, and mounted scenery are hung.

grips: Stage hands who shift the scenery.

groundplan (floor plan): The scaled-down drawing (blueprint) of the set containing all set information—exits, entrances measurements, etc.

ham: A term used to designate the type of artificial actor who generally overplays his part.

harmony: In a musical number, voice parts which are sung with the melody creating a richer, fuller texture of sound. (Opposite of unison singing.)

heavy: The villain of the play.

hero: The character who gets the sympathy of the audience—the "good guy."

heroine: The female counterpart of the hero.

hold: To remain static during a laugh or applause or to stress a tense dramatic moment.

hold book: To prompt, or in individual cases, simply to "hear lines."

house: Generally used to refer to the audience. Before the curtain goes up, a "good house" signifies a large number of paid admissions. After the curtain is up, it means an appreciative and responsive audience.

house lights: Lights in the theatre that illuminate the house (seating area) and are controlled by the lighting crew.

improvisation: Acting without a written script; creating the plot and dialogue as one performs.

ingenue: The actress who plays naïve parts.

juvenile: An actor who plays youthful roles.

kill: To eliminate. In theatre terms, "kill" the lights means to turn them off, "kill" the music means to stop it.

lash line: A short rope tied to each flat piece of scenery and used to bind the set.

lead: The principal part in a play.

left: Left from the standpoint of the actor. (To the audience's right.)

libretto: The term used to indicate the book (dialogue and lyrics) of a musical.

lift it: To enliven a scene by increasing the tempo and raising the pitch.

lighten it: To make a speech less emphatic by more speed, higher key or any other combination.

line: A row of words within any given set of dialogue. Sometimes used to refer to a whole speech.

lobby: Area of the theatre plant containing ticket booths, rest rooms and other audience service facilities.

lyrics: The words to a song.

make-up: Paint and powder, wigs, crepe hair, putty, mascara, etc., used to obtain facial effects on the stage.

mask: To conceal someone or something from the sight of a part or all of the audience. (In make-up it may refer to a facial covering.)

meter: In musical terms, the time signature of the song (how the beats of music are grouped by measures into strong and weak beats). Example: 2/4 time has a march feel and 3/4 time, a waltz feel.

monologue: A single speech from a drama spoken by a single individual actor.

mug: To overplay a part facially.

offstage: Backstage, but not on stage.

onstage: In view of the audience.

orchestration: In a musical, referring to the instruments which the composer has written the music for and the actual music itself. A show might be "orchestrated" for piano, bass and drums or for full wind orchestra.

overture: Instrumental music played by the orchestra before the opening of the curtain on *Act I* of a musical.

pantomime: Acting without words, using the body only.

part: 1. A role in a play or 2. The script containing the speeches and cues of any single role.

physicalization: The mannerisms and physical traits actors use to portray their character. This also includes how they manifest emotions.

pickup rehearsal: Rehearsals held during a long run of a show to keep the production sharp between performances.

picturization: A grouping of actors to create a dramatic effect. (Also referred to as composition.)

pin spot: A small spotlight used to accent a single point on the stage. Useful for supplying light to play dramatic scenes on a stage which is not sufficiently lit. Also used for special effects.

pit: Short for orchestra pit, the area below the playing area down front where the orchestra sits. In theatres without a built-in pit, the orchestra is often positioned off to one side.

"places": The order to stand by preparatory to the raising of the curtain, after the stage is cleared.

playbill: The program for the production containing cast information, advertising, etc.

playwright: The author of a play.

plot: 1. The story of the play or 2. The diagrammatic layout or scheme for lighting, offstage effects, properties, etc., or 3. The list of costumes, properties, etc., scene by scene.

plug: To reiterate or reemphasize a point already made.

point: To emphasize a speech or action.

practical: Working, as contrasted with "fake." A practical light switch, for example, is one that actually is connected to an onstage lamp.

production number: The large, showy numbers in a musical which often feature the entire company in song and dance. Most major musicals contain several production numbers.

projection: 1. Using the voice in such a way as to be heard clearly or 2. Referring to the set, an image shown on a screen or other flat surface.

prompt: To hold the book on the play (during rehearsal) and see to it that the actors deliver the correct lines. When the actor falters and needs help he requests "line" and the prompter feeds him the correct line.

prop table: A table in the backstage area where props are set and kept during performance. The property manager is in charge of this table.

property (prop): Any movable object that is necessary to the action of the play. Those which are carried by the actors (hand props) should generally be kept by them on their own responsibility. The actor should make a list of them, noting the acts in which their use is necessary, and check the list before each entrance. Other properties are the responsibility of the prop person, who collects them after each act, and checks them before each rise of the curtain.

proscenium: The arch that frames the proscenium stage.

proscenium theatre: Theatre presented where the audience views the play from only one side. A proscenium theatre is generally divided into four sections: lobby, house, stage and backstage.

readthrough: The rehearsal where the cast reads through the show for the first time.

reprise: The second or third occurence of a song in the show is called a reprise.

revue: A musical production highlighting songs from several different musicals.

right: Right from the standpoint of the actor (to the audience's left).

royalty: The fee to the publisher or author for the privilege of presenting a copyrighted play.

scene: A division of an act. In ordinary discussion, "scene" is used to refer to any well-defined episode in a play.

score: The bound book of music for a musical. There is a conductor's score, piano score, etc.

scrim: Large seamless gauze or mesh curtain generally stretched tight between top and bottom battens. Used for special effects. When lit from behind it appears transparent and from in front, opaque.

script: The text of a play.

segue: To go directly from one musical number to another without stopping.

set: 1. To prepare the stage for the play or 2. A unit of scenery inside of which the action of the play takes place.

sides: Scripts which do not contain the entire dialogue, rather, each character's lines and the cue lines which lead into each speech.

sightlines: Lines of vision from various places in the house—far right, left, the back row or balcony and the front row. The set designer designs, and positions the set so that areas "offstage" which are not supposed to be viewed by the audience can not be seen.

spike the set: To mark, usually with small pieces of tape, the exact spot where movable set pieces and furniture are to be positioned onstage. This aids the set crew and ensures that the pieces are in exactly the same spot each time for lighting purposes.

spot (follow spot): A movable light usually thrown from the balcony to bring one or more individual actors into prominent relief.

stall: To fill time, by improvisation, during an unforeseen delay.

steal: To distract the attention of the audience from the desired focus. Any uncalled-for movement or undesignated business is liable to do this. Sometimes a minor character is said to "steal the show" simply because the excellence of his performance overshadows the principals.

straight: Normal and natural. The opposite of "character" in referring to parts. To "play it straight" means to avoid mannerisms and the excessive dramatization of a role.

strike: The term used to signify the removal of a piece of stage furniture or scenery. To "strike" a chair is to take it off the stage. To "strike the set" is to dismantle the scene completely.

strips: A border of lights hung vertically in the wings.

tableau curtain: The type of draw curtain that is gathered up in loose loops and draped on each side, instead of simply parting in the middle.

tag: The last line of the play.

take a bow: To acknowledge the applause of the audience. (NEVER done in the middle of a scene.)

take stage: To assume the most prominent position in a scene, usually by moving to downstage, or centerstage. Sometimes the term refers to an actor giving himself more freedom of movement.

tempo: In musical terms, tempo is the speed of the song and in a scene it refers to the speed of the dialogue and action of a scene.

theme: The main idea to be proven by the action of the drama.

throw it away: To toss off a speech without stress. Useful in connection with speeches that are of commentary character and require no form of reply.

thrust stage: A theatre design with elements of both arena and proscenium staging. Usually a raised playing area where the audience views the action from three sides as if the apron section of a proscenium stage was built out into the house.

understudy: An actor who learns the part of another actor to replace him in the event that he is unable to perform.

unison: All voices on the same melody line, no harmony.

unit set: A type of set where one basic piece of scenery stays onstage for the entire production and smaller set pieces are arranged and rearranged, added or taken off.

up: Away from the audience.

upstage: Toward the rear of the stage set. In relation to another actor, being away from the footlights. One actor is said to "upstage" another actor if he remains upstage of him during a scene, thus necessitating the other actors turning his back to the audience when he speaks. (Also, the upstage actor tends to draw the focus.)

vamping: Repeating a few bars of music until singers or dancers are in place.

wagon: A rolling set piece which is used in drop or unit set staging.

walk-on: A minor part without lines.

warning: A preliminary cue for an entrance or an offstage effect.

wing: 1. A space on either side of the stage set or 2. A flat used to mask on the sides of a stage when the set is not completely enclosed. An actor "waiting in the wings" is ready for an entrance from the side.

work lights: Lights which illuminate the area behind the curtain including backstage an downstage areas. Usually regular wattage incandescent or fluorescent lights, they produce less heat and can be used when stage lighting isn't necessary.

Index